THE EPISTLE TO THE PHILIPPIANS
and
THE EPISTLE TO THE COLOSSIANS

NEW TESTAMENT FOR SPIRITUAL READING

Edited by
John L. McKenzie S.J.

THE EPISTLE TO THE PHILIPPIANS

JOACHIM GNILKA

THE EPISTLE TO THE COLOSSIANS

FRANZ MUSSNER

HERDER AND HERDER

1971
HERDER AND HERDER NEW YORK
232 Madison Avenue, New York 10016

Original editions: *Der Brief an die Philipper,* 1969, and *Der Brief an die Kolosser,* 1965, edited by Wolfgang Trilling in cooperation with Karl Hermann Schelkle and Heinz Schürmann, Düsseldorf, Patmos-Verlag.

Translated by R. A. Wilson.

Nihil Obstat: JOHN M. T. BARTON, STD., LSS., Censor

Imprimatur: ✠ VICTOR GUAZELLI, VG
Westminster 9 November 1970

Library of Congress Catalog Card Number: 70-77601

Printed in the Republic of Ireland by Cahill & Co. Limited

PREFACE

Two of the smaller epistles of Paul are presented here; both are said to be written from some imprisonment, which is generally thought to be connected with the narrative of Acts 21—28. This connection is not certainly established. In fact a number of modern scholars are inclined to attribute Colossians to "the school of Paul" rather than to Paul himself. Philippians is one of the more personal of the epistles; Colossians, on the contrary, is one of the more impersonal, except in the conclusion. By speaking of some of the epistles as the work of "the school of Paul" critics do not intend to deny any part of Paul in the production of these epistles. Certain features of style and content indicate that the personal activity of Paul in composition was not the same in all the epistles. Some may have been written by his associates at his commission, and others may have been continuations of the Pauline tradition.

The two epistles at first glance may seem unrelated. If the church of Philippi had particular problems, they are presented with too much subtlety for the modern reader. If it was a problem of church unity, the problem is certainly treated with less seriousness than the problems of unity at Corinth. At Colossae, on the other hand, the problem is clearly some false doctrine; this doctrine is difficult to identify, and the terms in which Paul rejects it are mild to a surprising degree. He spoke of the Judaizers with much more vigor; and perhaps it is more accurate to say that Paul thought of the doctrine as dangerous or useless rather than "false." In the apostolic church doctrines were not labeled with the precision which theologians acquired in later centuries.

Yet for different reasons Paul arrives at the same positive theme in both epistles; and this theme, the centrality of Christ, is the basic and the characteristic proposition of Pauline theology. In Philippians the centrality of Christ is seen and presented in a way rarely found elsewhere in the Pauline epistles, and nowhere at such length. Christ is placed at the center of the personal life of the individual Christian. This does not mean merely as a model; Christ gives meaning and value to the life and destiny of the individual Christian, and there is no hope for the Christian apart from Christ. The idea of "model" is suggested in the hymn to Christ, now generally thought to be quoted from early Christian worship and not composed by Paul (2:6–11). This passage does not suggest the "imitation" of Christ in the usual sense; Paul does not tell the Philippians to imitate Christ, but to grasp his mind, his attitude. As some commentators have pointed out, the imitation of Christ is not within the reach of believers. But the attitude of Christ towards the Father and his fellow man and his judgments of the values of life and the world can be shared, and in their perspective one will make decisions in one's personal life.

The centrality of Christ in Colossians is paralleled only in Ephesians, which with Colossians is regarded as a product of the school of Paul, largely because of this common doctrinal emphasis. The doctrine which Paul addresses may have been an early and relatively harmless form of Gnosticism. The numerous forms of this early heresy all had in common the multiplication of intermediary being and grades of being between God and redeemed man. Such theories easily imperiled the unique mediation of Christ; and Paul even warns against the cult of the angels. Elsewhere he accepts Jewish angelology without comment. The mediation of Christ in Colossians, however, is not limited to his death and resurrection. Christ appears as a cosmic figure, central in creation as he is in redemption. In creation headship is given him, and he is the objective towards which creation tends as its fulfillment. In Ephesians it is stated more clearly than in Colossians that the fullness of creation in Christ has not yet been reached. This does not imply that anything is lacking in the saving act of God in Christ, but that the reign of God is not yet total in creation. When it becomes effective, then the head and the body grow to their eschatological fullness. From different premises Paul arrives at very similar conclusions in Philippians 3:20 and in Colossians 3:1–4. Realized eschatology could hardly be stated more emphatically; with reference to the teachers of Colossae, it is clear that those whose life is heavenly have no need to pass through the intermediate grades of Gnostic salvation.

The modern reader's belief in the centrality of Christ is not threatened by Gnostics or Judaizers but by other threats more subtle than these. As much as the early Christians, he finds it difficult to think of himself as living on the heavenly plane. Paul cannot speak to us about the centrality of Christ unless we are willing to listen to him thoughtfully and to examine our condition in the world as he asked the Philippians and the Colossians to consider theirs. He seemed to think that an understanding faith in the centrality of Christ would enable us to judge true and false values.

JOHN L. MCKENZIE.

The Epistle to the Philippians

INTRODUCTION

The apostle Paul had grown particularly fond of the church of Philippi, and there may have been several reasons for this situation. Above all the Philippians had been outstanding from the first by their obedience and loyalty towards their apostle. The church of Philippi, it will be remembered, had been established by Paul, but had soon to rely upon itself in the midst of a heathen environment. The apostle had set out for new cities, and the newly founded church of Philippi was put to the test of existing on its own. Could the seed that had been sown in it strike root and survive, or would it be stifled in the weeds of heresy that surrounded it? Not only had the Philippians themselves come through this test, but they had clearly also understood that once one had achieved faith in the gospel oneself, one had the duty to do something to promote this gospel. A church is safe from the danger of falling away and finally collapsing only when it remains lively and active.

The Philippians had yet another distinction, for they were the first Pauline church in Europe. There is probably only one church in Europe older than Philippi, that of Rome. On his second missionary journey, Paul, with Silas and Timothy, crossed from Asia Minor to Macedonia. He had previously worked only in Asia Minor (see Acts 13—14). But from the first he must have cherished the wish to carry the message of Christ into the Greek world. His missionary activity in Philippi ended with a clash, and had to be broken off before its conclusion, when the city authorities proceeded against the missionaries and drove them out of the city (see Acts 16:11ff.; 1 Thess. 2:2). Paul was well aware that the young church was still in need of supervision. He was also thankful that his work had not remained fruitless, indeed, it had borne rich fruit.

It is important in reading any letter to have an approximate idea of the situation of its writer. This is reflected in his statements, plans, and hopes. Paul wrote the Epistle to the Philippians while in prison. He frequently mentions his chains, and considers the possibility of his death. Thus we are dealing with one of what are known as the "Captivity Epistles." Here Paul's soul, his striving, his desires, and above all his faith are especially evident, and this is what makes this epistle so valuable. It has been called the most personal of all Paul's epistles. When we read these lines we should always remember the miserable position in which Paul found himself. The prisons of the ancient world were anything but humane, and the food was wretched. One would expect in view of this to find Paul complaining about the guards, about the uncertainty of the future, and about the restrictions. There is nothing of the sort. Paul understands his situation wholly on the basis of Christian faith, and does not merely surmount it by his faith, but makes it a glorious testimony of faith. We see the greatness of the slave of Christ, yet it is not a greatness remote from us, and unattainable, but within human compass, real, tangible, and capable of being imitated. Anyone who must suffer and bear trials for the sake of the faith can find a standard of faith in the suffering apostle. Paul's prison, where this epistle was written, was in Ephesus, the major city of Asia Minor, along the east coast of the Aegean Sea. It was only an eight-day journey from Philippi.

What is the purpose of the epistle? First of all, it gives information about Paul's present situation. But it is the church that he has in mind, and it is from the church's point of view that he considers his own fate. In this attitude, in which his own personal concerns are overshadowed by his preoccupation with the church to which he is writing, we can see the sincerity and honesty of his apostolic, missionary commitment. He had to remember that he might never see Philippi again, and therefore had to concern himself for its future. The building up of the church, its standing in the world, and its salvation are the main pastoral purposes of this epistle. Because they are so general, the epistle can still be read with value by every age and every church. Paul also makes plans for the future. But they are full of uncertainty.

OUTLINE

CONCLUDING REQUESTS AND DISCUSSION (4 : 2–20)

I. Euodia and Syntyche (4 : 2–3)

II. Joy, peace, and perseverance (4 : 4–9)

III. The apostle's thanksgiving (4 : 10–20)

The Close of the Letter (4:21–23)

CONCLUSION (4 : 21–23)

THE OPENING OF THE LETTER
(1:1–2)

THE LETTERHEAD
(1:1–2)

[1]*Paul and Timothy, servants of Christ Jesus, to all the saints in Christ Jesus who are at Philippi, with the bishops and deacons:* [2]*Grace to you and peace from God our Father and the Lord Jesus Christ.*

Apostolic epistles are letters full of authority and responsibility. Yet, though Paul felt the weight of responsibility for his churches, he does not describe himself to the Philippians as an apostle, but rather as a " servant, a slave of Christ Jesus." He does not use the title of " apostle," to which reverence would be due, but places himself on the same level as Timothy, his assistant. At that time the slave was for everyone a familiar, everyday fact of life. There may have been quite a number of slaves, in fact, amongst those who heard the epistle read. A slave has a master, and Paul saw himself as enslaved to the *kyrios* (lord or master) Jesus Christ. In this way he removed the stigma of being a slave. Paul has submitted himself completely to Christ Jesus as his Lord, so that he is now his slave and servant.

The same is true of Timothy. This shows that for Paul the name of a slave is an honorable one. Not every person is entitled to it, but only those among the faithful who have accepted a task and responsibility in missionary work. The others are " saints." This word too sounds strange, but it does not signify that the " saints " have already overcome sin completely in their own lives, or that there is no longer any evil among them. That they are " saints in Christ Jesus " describes the situation exactly. It is not for anything in themselves that they are called saints. It has been brought about by Christ. He has drawn them to himself. They now belong to him. They have been sanctified by baptism and faith. Belonging to Christ in this way imposes an obligation upon them, for now they, who are saints, have a duty to become holy. A Christian is constantly called to become better: to become what he is.

In the church of Philippi there are " bishops and deacons." Paul greets them separately. It is certain that this greeting is for those who have undertaken *pastoral responsibility* for others, thus showing that the ministry is coming into being. We must remember that during his lifetime and ministry Paul himself carried full responsibility for his churches. But he had to take thought for the future, for a time when he would no longer be with them, and also for the time when he was on missionary journeys and was at work elsewhere. The twofold " hierarchy " of *episkopoi* and deacons was collegial in the way it worked. A number of individuals held equal authority and responsibility in brotherly concord. The word *" episkopos "* is the origin of the word " bishop."

The introduction to the letter closes with a liturgical greeting. The people of the church are to hear and accept his words in the peace and grace of God and Christ.

THE BODY OF THE LETTER
(1:3—4:20)

PAUL AND THE CHURCH

(1:3–26)

Prayer of Thanksgiving for the Philippians (1:3–8)

3 *I thank my God in all my remembrances of you,* 4 *always in*
every prayer of mine for you all making my prayer with joy,
5 *thankful for your partnership in the gospel from the first day*
until now. 6 *And I am sure that he who began a good work in*
you will bring it to completion at the day of Jesus Christ. 7 *It is*
right for me to feel thus about you all, because I hold you in my
heart, for you are all partakers with me of grace, both in my
imprisonment and in the defense and confirmation of the gospel.
8 *For God is my witness, how I yearn for you all with the*
affection of Christ Jesus.

Paul begins what he has to say to the church with a prayer. His heart is full of thanksgiving when he remembers the Philippians. He knows that the church is kept in the care and protection of God, but he commends them nevertheless to God who protects them. Pastoral care is also a matter of prayer, indeed it is primarily a matter of prayer, and it is certainly at fault if it is not sustained by the prayer of the pastor. The single word " always " describes this attitude. Unceasing prayer is not something that is to be taken literally, but should govern the life of a Christian as an attitude of prayer exercised towards God. Paul's position before God is something he feels personally: he speaks of " my

God." But he does not exploit or misuse the personal relationship he has achieved with God. Rather, it is the opportunity which makes it possible for him to give thanks. Anyone who can give thanks, and feels thanksgiving as a primary need, deserves to be called great. Paul is in prison and gives thanks!

Thanksgiving is accompanied by joy. The joy of a captive cannot spring from natural sources. It flows from God, and sweeps over Paul when he thinks of the Philippians, "you all." No one is left out. Physical distance, affectionate memories, and the longing of separation make Paul conscious of an obligation to each individual. He knows them all personally, and remembers each one. Thus he can pray for each of them. The church cannot have been very large. The very personal nature of his prayer extends to the church as a whole.

But he does not pray for them because they have an obligation to him. Their obligation is to the gospel. This gospel is a living force. It has not yet become a book, but is the life-giving word that is preached. Before the gospel was put into words, Paul set forth his gospel, and founded and built up churches through its power. The Philippians also owed their present life of faith to this word. But their part in the gospel also went further, for they have committed themselves to its preaching. Not only are they open to receive, they are ready to give. This has been so from the very first. Their receptiveness, for which Paul can thank God, is due to the fact that they have understood the inner significance of the spiritual power of the word, which must be passed on, and which reveals its power only when it is passed on.

Looking back on all this, Paul says that he is certain of God's work in them. This sureness comes from prayer, and is a trust in God. Paul has always committed all his strength, all his time, and his whole person to the preaching of the gospel and the consolidation of the churches. His activity and versatility might give the impression to an outside observer that he plans to do a great deal, perhaps everything, himself. His restless activity comes from the conviction that God begins and perfects everything. He calls the task of the preacher and the setting up of churches a work. But he does not regard it as his work, but as the work of God and Christ. His part is merely that of a laborer continuing the work of the Lord. Thus he can remain sure, even when he has suddenly and unexpectedly to cease his labor for a while, that the work will go on.

Most human work leaves behind it the impression of something incomplete and fragmentary, especially when many plans are left unrealized, and many projects never get beyond words and committees. It is God who sets the limit and lays down the path. Paul is sure that God will bring his work to completion. And what began in Philippi was God's work.

Paul has this exalted memory of all of them. He speaks to the Philippians like a father to his children. He holds his beloved church in his heart as a father holds his children. But now at last he must speak of his imprisonment. Hitherto he has not stopped even for a moment to refer to it, so much are his own person and his private affairs overshadowed by the affairs of the church. It is characteristic that when he now mentions his captivity, rather as an aside, he relates it to the church and the gospel. His imprisonment is not a shame, an irritation, a burden, or a dishonor; it is grace. It seems to Paul to be almost something holy, and the Philippians should call it such.

But they have done so already. They have already made it clear that they have perceived the true significance of his imprisonment and outward shame. Consequently they partake in his grace.

The fate of the apostle is bound up with that of the gospel. What happens to the one happens to the other. The gospel is imprisoned with him, but by his defense the gospel is also defended and confirmed. His own person does not matter. As if in a dialogue with God he swears to his love for them, for all of them. The sincerity of his bond with each individual must be affirmed in the sight of God. Here he is placing himself under judgment as a pastor, but Paul has a clear, transparent conscience. Love is the only feeling he has when he remembers them.

Let us reflect for a moment on how the church of Philippi was actually composed: rich people, and many of the poor, old and young, sick and well people afflicted like us with all the human weaknesses. It may seem exaggerated and humanly impossible for Paul to be equally fond of all of them. Yet it is true. For someone else is at work in Paul, Christ Jesus himself. Through him Christ Jesus acts and loves. In this passage we can see the very essence of what it means to be a Christian, something incomprehensible, unnatural, offensive to the unaided understanding, but to faith the very central meaning of life.

Paul Prays for the Philippians (1:9–11)

9*And it is my prayer that your love may abound more and more,*
with knowledge and all discernment, 10*so that you may approve*
what is excellent, and may be pure and blameless for the day of
Christ, 11*filled with the fruits of righteousness which come*
through Jesus Christ, to the glory and praise of God.

The thanksgiving is followed by petition. This is the right order that man should follow in the entreaty that he makes in his prayer to God. What Paul asks for the church is love. This ought to grow, because it is always able to increase. A Christian church should be a community in which all the people are bound together by love. But their love should also be effective towards those outside. Of course, it is possible to speak of love and affection in many different ways, and even quite casually. In rare moments of blissful emotion, a person may have an urge to embrace all humanity with its millions, but what does that signify? Love can be deformed into a mask for the egotism of a couple or a group. It needs the critical insight that destroys self-deception. Love must be perceptive. Love is not a frenzy that passes; for a Christian it is an attitude that must endure, and in which he has to endure. Love is authenticated and verified in little everyday things, and in encounters where perhaps we would have preferred conflict instead. Thus love must be accompanied by discernment.

Paul's prayer turns to an ethical appeal, to exhortation. He does not give concrete instructions, but sets out a general principle that covers everything. The Doctor of the Church, Augustine, was later to proclaim: "Love, and do what you will." If we compare this to Paul's exhortation, we might sum up by saying that the apostle's call is: "Love, and do what really matters." What matters is to *do* it. For action has to be taken at the time it offers itself, and a missed opportunity can be blameworthy.

There is an urgency in all of Paul's ethical exhortation, because it is related to the day of Christ. The church of Paul's time lived in the consciousness that the end of time and history was pressing in, and the faithful were preparing themselves for this final moment. Our world view is a different one, but the claim of time, which is at our disposal in a strictly limited way, is no less strong. It has remained, and in the face of the crises of world history is even more powerful. The day of Christ signifies liberation and redemption finally and forever. This day is still to come, and we know it, for we cannot provide it ourselves, and the progress of the centuries, past and to come, withholds it from us. So the Christian church must now look forward to that "day" just as much as she did in her first years under the guidance of Paul.

There will be a time of trial in the sight of God. It must find us pure and blameless. But here again it is the deed that matters, not what we have succeeded in not doing; for we are to be justified by the fruits of righteousness which we bring with us. We do not create them ourselves, and even the first impulse does not come from us. The fruit comes through Jesus Christ. For in Christ we have been made worthy to praise and give glory to God.

The Progress of the Gospel (1:12–18)

12 *I want you to know, brethren, that what has happened to me*
has really served to advance the gospel, 13 *so that it has become*
known throughout the whole praetorian guard and to all the
rest that my imprisonment is for Christ; 14 *and most of the*
brethren have been made confident in the Lord because of my
imprisonment, and are much more bold to speak the word of
God without fear. 15 *Some indeed preach Christ from envy and*
rivalry, but others from good will. 16 *The latter do it out of love,*
knowing that I am but here for the defense of the gospel; 17 *the*
former proclaim Christ out of partisanship, not sincerely but
thinking to afflict me in my imprisonment. 18 *What then? Only*

that in every way, whether in pretense or in truth, Christ is proclaimed; and in that I rejoice.

Paul writes from prison. The Philippians knew this, only we too must realize it. Paul now turns to himself, or, more precisely, by talking of himself, he comes to the gospel. The outward impression given by his situation might be described as follows. His missionary activity in Asia Minor, with its center at Ephesus, had been brought to an abrupt end by his arrest. It seemed to be finished. The progress of the gospel seemed to have been met with a catastrophe. The churches were asking how they could make further progress, and even whether they could make any at all. Paul gives a consoling answer from prison: against all expectation the gospel has gone forward, both in prison and on the outside, both where the apostle now was and in the church where he was held in Ephesus.

Paul thus interprets his situation in the light of faith, and speaks of a revelation of his chains, in that it has become known that his imprisonment is for Christ. Even as a prisoner the apostle of Christ has a task of supreme importance to fulfill. The commission with which he has been sent forth still holds, even when he is chained and bound. There is still room to work, and an opportunity to bear witness. Shortly before, Paul must have had an even more dramatic opportunity, and he is probably referring to a public trial in the courthouse, the praetorium. We do not learn what the result was for him personally of this appearance before the governor of the city. He does not think it worth mentioning in his letter, and it may be that he left it to whomever carried the letter to make it known by word of mouth. The only thing of importance is that Christ has been made known by Paul's imprisonment, his imprisonment in

Christ. This comes about by itself. Paul knows this. The word he spoke before his judges and the whole assembly is being carried on, and is travelling farther than the narrow limits of that moment and place.

But the apostle's appearance in court had results other than mere personal consequences. The local church must have had to suffer as a result of his imprisonment. It had become dangerous to preach the gospel. Perhaps this was the first time the faithful had become aware of this fact to such an extent. The outcome was dejection, fear, gloom, and timidity. But Paul's bold demeanor in the praetorium, which they must have known about, and which they must have waited anxiously to hear about, brought about a change. Courage is infectious, and one confession of faith brings forth another. Most of the brethren were inspired by his witness, and once again dared to preach even though it was now dangerous.

But Paul is not satisfied merely with preaching. There is preaching with insincere and base motives. Not only does he see through this activity, as a wise man of the world, but he does not hesitate to denounce it. For it is always harmful to a congregation, and to the church as a whole, when abuses within are covered up or even excused. The more they are ignored, the more successfully their evil spreads. Envy and rivalry have broken down the common mind that the preachers in Ephesus should have had. Christ is being preached with ulterior motives. The situation is characterized in concrete terms, but there is no immediate mention of a motive. Only when we read on do we learn that Paul is in the middle of this dispute. It is his person and his imprisonment which shows which side people are on. His imprisonment reveals the honesty or doubtfulness of their intentions.

Christian life needs times of threat and peril to know itself fully. A hidden Christianity can very soon turn stale. Peace must not be a false peace. The acceptance of suffering, hurt, privation through the deeper understanding of faith, and the interpretation of them in the light of faith, shows whether a person's Christianity is genuine. Underlying Paul's suffering is a destiny given by God. God put him there for the defense of the gospel. That is how he, and part of the church in Ephesus, see the situation. Others deny that his imprisonment has this inner meaning. And so they want to make it unbearable for him.

This is Paul's temptation. It is certainly a strong one, on a level with his greatness. His temptation does not lie in his having to suffer, go hungry, endure, freeze, and submit to mockery. He knows his destiny. But for believers like himself to dispute his destiny cuts him to the quick. They must have done it from cowardice. They imagined they were safe if they disassociated themselves from Paul in prison. The test to which Paul is put by his imprisonment is that of remaining true to the significance of a wretched situation when doubt has been cast upon it. But the joy that breaks through at the end of his comments shows that Paul has not been led astray. What some see as an offense and a foolishness, he regards as a means for the revelation of Christ, intended as such by God.

Paul even includes his opponents explicitly in his rejoicing, for in spite of everything they are proclaiming Christ. The magnanimity that he shows here should not be thought of as tolerance. He is not talking about people who have spread a false doctrine. Paul is able to make this judgment because he keeps his own personal affairs, or things that can be regarded as his own personal affairs and are seen as such by his opponents, quite separate from the one thing with which he is really concerned. His disregard of himself cannot be exaggerated. It is utterly objective, but not in an inhuman sense, for it is associated with great emotion. The root of this emotion is his joy, not of course at the evil that is being done, but at the goodness that can still be found in perverse and repugnant actions.

Life or Death (1:19–24)

19 *Yes, and I shall rejoice. For I know that through your prayers*
and the help of the Spirit of Jesus Christ this will turn out for
my deliverance, 20 *as it is my eager expectation and hope that I*
shall not be at all ashamed, but that with full courage now as
always Christ will be honored in my body, whether by life or
by death. 21 *For to me to live is Christ, and to die is gain.* 22 *If it is*
to be life in the flesh, that means fruitful labor for me. Yet which
I shall choose I cannot tell. 23 *I am hard pressed between the two.*
My desire is to depart and be with Christ, for that is far better.
24 *But to remain in the flesh is more necessary on your account.*

The expression of his joy leads on to the next passage. It is the hidden force at work in the present, and so too will it determine the future. Paul has no fear for his own personal future, to which he now turns. He believes he will be delivered. He expresses his confidence in the words of Job: "This will turn out for my deliverance."

In fact, Paul does have cause to compare himself with the patient Job. But we see what his particular view of the future is when we realize what he means by deliverance. It seems obvious that he is thinking of the deliverance of his life from prison and the executioner's axe. But this is not what Paul has in mind, as the words that follow make clear. Deliverance here means the same as ultimate salvation. He has no doubt of this. But even an apostle can be tempted. In his time of trial he relies on two things, the prayer of the church and the help of the Spirit of the Lord. The church has to pray for its pastor. This is much better than criticism. The genuine unity between them is sustained by the work of the Spirit. The whole of the work, life, struggles, and suffering of Paul has been and is directed towards Christ. His whole existence, his whole bodily being in this mortal life, is devoted to the service of the Lord, so that his bodily life can become the place of the epiphany of Christ before the world. It will be so however much time and whatever possibilities are available to him in the future. He cannot yet tell how much or what these may be, but he shows how wide his field of expectations is in the alternatives he gives of life or death. In both cases, as always in the past, Christ will be visibly glorified in him, the apostle. If *life* is allotted to him, this will take place as before in the apostolic work in which he works and triumphs and suffers. If death comes his way, he will become like his Lord, and be in a position to make his Lord's suffering visible to the world. The apostle is ready to follow Christ to the very end. But Christ himself must sustain him. He cannot let him fall or be put to shame.

Paul is faced with the possibility of life or death, with the basic questions of human existence: What is life? What is death? In the face of death he gives an answer which is a testimony to the greatness of his faith in Christ and his love of Christ. Life is Christ. We do not know which is subject and which is predicate in this sentence: whether it states that Christ is life, or that life is Christ. Life and Christ belong so closely together. The link between them is an exclusive one: there is life only where Christ is. The consequence is that to die is gain. Paul states in the next sentence what the gain is, but it is already clear that life is a word which goes beyond earthly limits. The possession of the life that is described here is not limited to this earth, so that death can lead to its true possession.

Does Paul become a fanatic? Is he rushing headlong towards death? Is he fleeing earthly life because it is intolerable to him? Not in the least. He has already described the alternative of life and death as a matter of indifference to him with regard to the glorification of Christ which is his task. Once again he emphatically defends life "in the flesh." If this is his lot, he obediently accepts it. His work is not yet finished. If he is allowed to go on living, he is being given a welcome opportunity to press on with the work allotted to him, of bearing fruit for Christ. This faces him with a personal choice. The decision is a difficult one, yet he demands it of himself. But is it really his affair to lay down which way he should take? In the spirit of prayer Paul breaks through the outward human situation and places himself before God, in whose sight he wishes his decision to be made. The Roman judges, in their dignity and power, are puppets in the hands of him whom Paul calls his God.

It is not easy to have a clear view of oneself in the sight of God. Paul's personal wish is opposed to the necessity of the situation. He is torn in two directions. His inner unease can be read between the lines. He has just said that to die is gain. He makes this statement even stronger. It is *far better* to depart and set out on the great journey. Paul knows where it leads: to communion with Christ, to *be with Christ*. He understands Christian existence and realizes it as existence in Christ. According to his preaching, communion with Christ is the root of the life of faith in this present age.

Paul also reflects upon death, something that he has rarely mentioned. The expectation of the coming of Christ far overshadows anything he has to say about death. But this does not mean that because the time of waiting for Christ is short, he intends to pass over it or not think about it. Death does not reduce human life to the existence of a shade in the underworld, which was what the Old Testament looked forward to. Nor must the dead wait until the last day brings them to life. The communion with Christ which they have gained in life by faith is not broken when they cross the threshold of death, but is intensified and made more blessed still. Paul is wary of expressing his view in concrete terms. He leaves existence beyond the boundary of earthly life as something inexpressible, and is content to promise that it is existence with Christ. But this is enough. In faith he surmounts the problem of death and so gives the only possible genuine answer to it.

Here he has given rein to his inner longing and allowed us an insight into his love for Christ. He now makes his final decision. Because the churches still need him, he must remain. In speaking in this way he is not treating himself as indispensable. One might suppose this if he were merely affirming his wish to remain because of his awareness of his own abilities. But he does not judge by what he is himself, but in the sight of God. He believes that he sees God's providence in the necessity for him to remain.

Confidence (1:25–26)

[25]*Convinced of this, I know that I shall remain and continue with you all, for your progress and joy in the faith,* [26]*so that in*

me you may have ample cause to glory in Christ Jesus, because of my coming to you again.

Understanding brings confidence. He is given to them, to all of them. He hopes to assist their progress, but also their joy. When he returns to them, that will be an occasion for them to glory. Paul says much in his epistles about glory and glorying. He knows, having learned it from his conflicts with the Jews and from his own past, that there is a false glorying. This trusts in its own achievement, its own deeds, its own excellence, in the *sarx* (the flesh). Such glorying is an illusion. It is useless and only does harm. But there is a saving and necessary glorying, which is glorying in Christ Jesus. In this kind of glorying, we acknowledge and praise the work that God himself has carried out, the deliverance that he has created. This glorying is the attitude the church and the apostle should have towards each other: that is, that they should glorify each other. Slander and exaggerated criticism poison the atmosphere. To recognize in others the work of Christ, represented here by the arrival of Paul, expected shortly, brings joy in the faith and a true unity.

EXHORTATION TO THE CHURCH (1:27—2:18)

Paul's epistles usually fall into two principal groups of material, the first is more doctrinal in substance, while the second contains exhortation, comfort, admonition, and encouragement. The usual order is varied in this epistle, insofar as the first part is filled with personal information—although we have seen that it goes beyond the purely personal as a result of the close link with the gospel. In the second part Paul returns to the normal order. He addresses the church directly.

Fight with One Mind for the Faith (1:27–30)

27 *Only let your manner of life be worthy of the gospel of Christ,*
so that whether I come and see you or am absent, I may hear of
you that you stand firm in one spirit, with one mind striving
side by side for the faith of the gospel, 28 *and not frightened in*
anything by your opponents. This is a clear omen to them of
their destruction, but of your salvation, and that from God.
29 *For it has been granted to you that for the sake of Christ you*
should not only believe in him but also suffer for his sake,
30 *engaged in the same conflict which you saw and now hear to*
be mine.

After expressing his confidence that it will soon be possible for him to visit the Philippians, he sees himself as already with them in the Spirit. He is an apostle speaking to his congregation. He reminds them once again of the gospel. The gospel conveyed to them has become the standard of their lives as Christians, and so it must always be. The church would not then be without the word. It is necessary for the maintenance of a congregation that the word should always be alive in its midst and should always be preached there. This must be a common concern. A characteristic of this admonition by Paul is that it appeals to all the church, in the common responsibility its members have for one another. Christian life cannot be brought to realization in secluded corners, shut off from others. It must always be orientated towards others, seeking to win them, concerned for them, and serving them.

Paul wishes in any case to be in contact with them, even if only by hearing about them. As a new church, certainly few in numbers, the Philippians had to hold their own before the world outside. To stand together, as they are always being exhorted, was essential for their very survival. They had already and inevitably learned that the life of faith is a conflict, but one in which the individual is always weak and is bound to succumb. Only the group, the community, is able to endure and survive.

Paul speaks of opponents. The Christian church must have seemed alien to many. It has been its fate from the very first to cause scandal and offense. This is its function, and it must expect it. If it did not give offense and settled for conventional compromises, went back on its claims or modified them, it would cease to be what it is. Its uniqueness is seen only when its members hold together, and offer each other help and assistance. The unity which must be the sign of the church is elevated by Paul into a sign in a double sense. It is a guarantee to the church of its salvation, but to its opponents it is a sign of their destruction. The concern for unity must be maintained even when there are no divisions. For it is a basic principle of community and church life, but to its opponents it is the seed of destruction. The church must not let itself be eroded away from outside. For if its opponents succeed in damaging its single-mindedness, the damage would be more than an outward one. Only unity brings salvation, eternal salvation.

The calling of believers is summed up by Paul in an expression which becomes almost a cliché with him: " for the sake of Christ "—to exist for the sake of Christ, as we have expanded it. The basis on which one's life is so orientated is that of faith. But for Paul faith is never a matter of theory, an intellectual game; it takes in the whole man. Man appreciates the comprehensive claim of faith when he has to suffer for his conviction. Thus Paul mentions faith before suffering. For there can be no meaningful obligation to suffer without the ability to have faith.

What is remarkable, however, is that Paul, looking at the misfortunes of the Philippians, which their fellow citizens must have brought upon them, places them on the same level as his own, even though they were by no means comparable. He explains to them that like him they should not merely accept privations for Christ's sake, but should know that they are God's grace. This is why suffering has been granted to them. God's gifts are peculiar to himself. And perhaps it needs time to pass from resistance or avoidance of suffering to the realization that it is grace that one has received.

Paul assures them that it is the same conflict which unites them with him in a special way. Even though his lot is now far more difficult than theirs, he includes their fate with his, for they are united with him not only because their struggle has the same goal, but also by the spiritual attitude with which they accept their suffering. He proposes himself to them as an example, and reminds them that it is not the first time that they have heard of the afflictions that have been laid upon him. When he was with them in Philippi he was engaged in the same conflict. It was a difficult one, and they know it. They should be edified by it, remembering the past and looking at his present situation.

Be of One Mind (2:1–4)

1So if there is any encouragement in Christ, any incentive of
love, any participation in the Spirit, any affection and sympathy,
2complete my joy by being of the same mind, having the same
love, being in full accord and of one mind. 3Do nothing from
selfishness or conceit, but in humility count others better than
yourselves. 4Let each of you look not only to his own interests,
but also to the interests of others.

A resolute attitude towards the world outside is genuine and stable only if all is well within. This passage contains a word that is characteristic of Paul's exhortation: *paraklesis.* But if it is translated " exhortation," its meaning is restricted, for it is wider than this. It ranges from comfort and consolation to encouragement and admonition, and embraces all the breadth, warmth, and liveliness of the words a pastor is able to utter to his congregation, and which he should be able to call upon. To avoid banality, its distinctive nature is preserved by the expression " encouragement in Christ." This must be filled with love, since it is sustained by the Spirit, who binds them together. The pointing finger of moral indignation is repelled. Only true unity makes true exhortation possible.

Because Paul's relationship to the church is that of a father to his children, he is glad that things are well with them spiritually. This is shown by the love they have for one another. Love is harmony, oneness, being of one soul and one mind. The need for ***agape,*** for love of this kind, is often enough proclaimed in the Christian church, but just as often it is discounted or overlooked. Instances of lack of love are regarded as of no account. People are inspired by things which are easier to grasp. The confusion of the letter and the spirit was a threat to the church as early as this time, and it is still a threat.

There have been instances of lack of love in the church of Philippi. Paul has heard of them. Lack of love is expressed in contentiousness and boasting. But love is humble; it counts others better than itself. Humility was something at which men in the ancient world were not very practiced. In the Greek world the word " humility " had a bad odor. It meant the same as a crawling attitude, servility, toadying. Such an attitude was alien to a free man, who despised it. But a Christian is humble before God above all because he knows that he has received and receives everything from him. And from his attitude towards God he achieves true humility before his fellow men, his brothers, by seeing in them the spark of God.

There are practical consequences in regarding one's fellow men in this way. People are concerned for their own good from self-love. But love brings a concern for the good of others, which is of as much value as one's own. Fine talk about love bears no fruit. It is witnessed to only in action.

The Path of Jesus (2:5–11)

5 *Have this mind among yourselves, which you have in Christ Jesus,*

[6]*who, though he was in the form of God, did not count equality with God a thing to be grasped,*

[7]*but emptied himself, taking the form of a servant, being born in the likeness of men.*

[8]*And being found in human form he humbled himself and became obedient unto death, even death on a cross.*

[9]*Therefore God has highly exalted him and bestowed on him the name which is above every name,*

[10]*that at the name of Jesus every knee should bow, in heaven and on earth,*

[11]*and every tongue confess that Jesus Christ is Lord, to the glory of God the Father.*

At this point Paul inserts a hymn about Christ into the text of the epistle. Several things indicate that he is not using his own words but has borrowed them: for Paul, these are strange words in a strange form of presentation—the breakdown of the lines into stanzas, for example. But the apostle makes the hymn his own. He does not simply quote it; he thinks it through, reflects on it, adds to it, and puts it in a context.

This context permits Paul to refer to the hymn which was sung in the church's liturgical gatherings. He has just spoken of the necessity of humility, that they should count others better than themselves and meet them with love. He passes to the hymn with the exhortation that they should have the same mind which is right in Christ Jesus. This phrase must be explained. It might be supposed that it simply points to Christ as an example, that one should be of the same mind as he. Paul's argument is different and more profound. He never tires in his epistles of explaining to the churches and reminding them that when they believed and were baptized, they entered into a new relationship to Christ and therefore to God. He tells them that they are now in Christ, under the saving rule of the *kyrios* (Lord) Christ. Under this rule there is a new law, the law which Christ revealed. This is what a Christian must always bear in mind. For to be in Christ is a substantive definition of what it is to be a Christian. Paul wishes to come back to this very essence of Christianity. He does so by means of the hymn.

The hymn has two stanzas which describe in splendid outline the path followed by Christ. This led from his existence with God before the world began, into the world of men, and back again to rule with God.

In the beginning the hymn seeks to express the inexpressible. There was one in the world of God who was himself in the form of God. This is not a watering down, and does not signify another deity, but asserts neither more nor less than that he who is spoken of here *is* God. But it is not the concern of the mythical language to describe the being of God or the relationship of this being who is like to God to God himself, but to give an account of the action which now starts from God.

Its sole motive is freedom. He was not forced or compelled to carry out this action, but did it of his own accord. He emptied himself. He gave himself up. This action is completely incomprehensible, and an equally paradoxical expression is used to describe this: he did not believe that he must hang on to his being like a booty, the fruits of a robbery. This would have been only what was to be expected. But something unexpected, incomprehensible, inexpressible happened: his emptying, his self-emptying.

The form of God is replaced by the *form of a servant*. He himself willed it. The contrast between God and a servant is appropriate to a difference vaster, more full of tension, more unbridgeable than can ever be imagined. It is a matter of accepting a knowledge of this in our bewilderment at it. But the contrast between God and a servant remains an enigma, because man is the natural opposite to God.

In fact the hymn is a solemn confession of praise at one fact, that God became man. The three phrases that repeat the idea have this single purpose, which they develop step by step. He became *true man,* not the illusion that the Docetists believed in. He made himself one of the multitude of mankind, and took on their form, their essential form, and his appearance palpably left no doubt that he was a man, and as man, a servant.

The form of a servant, which is given as the first aim of the process of self-emptying, needs to be elucidated. Its meaning derives from its connection with the phrase " the form of God," and this relationship shows clearly the abyss which only he could bridge. But it means more than this. Human existence is understood as servile existence, as slavery. Within the framework of mythical thought there are powers, supra-terrestrial, cosmic powers, which rule man and force him under their yoke. If we remove the mythical element of this concept, we are left with a suggestion that life is subject to blind chance. Where is its meaning, its central significance? In the myth of the cosmic powers life seems to be a cruel game played by enslaving forces. Fear and uncertainty are the expression of this consciousness. The One who is free enters such a world.

He reveals obedience. Obedience is the law we have noted above, and it determines the form of Christian existence. Of course, the obedience of this One is so great as to be beyond imitation. This is so because he comes from the world of God, from whence no one has come as he has. The obedience he shows and lives is something self-contained and separate from the world and man. The connection between the two, which can only be God, is not mentioned. The freedom of such obedience is stronger than any free obedience that is possible for men. The self-emptying is followed by self-humiliation. It goes so far as obedience unto death. Death is the final stage in a path undertaken in freedom. Only in this way can death too be a free act. Yet it is death which shows that he has really become one of us. For death is the fate that unites all men, regardless of their origin or race, their birth or opinions. Not that all are alike in death, but in death they all come together. The different paths which have led them over the heights and depths of this world join in death. Whoever dies is human. To understand that the death of this One is a free act is possible only with a knowledge of his pre-history.

Nothing can be imagined to be farther from God than death. No further word is needed to plumb the full depths of what this way meant. That this was a death on the cross comes as additional information. Here the hand of Paul is visible; it was he who added this phrase. The cross is at the center of his gospel, and signifies the death of Christ as a saving death. "The word of the cross is folly to those who are perishing, but to us who are being saved it is the power of God" (1 Cor. 1:18). It is the sole ground for glorying which the apostle permits himself (Gal. 6:14). When he expounds and proclaims the death of Christ by recalling that it was death on the cross, he is not intending to increase the horror of it, but to signify that it brings salvation.

In the second part of the hymn it is now God who acts. Along the path of self-emptying and humiliation it was the other alone who acted. But whereas God was always present as the point of reference of his obedience, it is now clearly stated that God is at work, and takes the initiative. This is directed towards the obedience that has been exercised. It is one of the earliest experiences of biblical religion that God brings down and raises up the righteous. As though in a test, the righteous one is submitted to the discipline of humiliation, so that when he has proved himself, he may be acknowledged by his God. This rule of exaltation following humiliation lives on in this hymn, but it is altered in a unique way. Here it is not a question of a moral test, or of God having humiliated a righteous person, but of the revelation of the obedience that only this One could freely exercise. The way chosen by this One, the way of self-humiliation, is unique, and therefore calls forth a unique response from God.

He exalted him who had emptied himself in death. We are used to hearing the message of Easter expressed in different words: that Jesus was raised on the third day, rose again, appeared to Cephas, and so on. Nothing of this is mentioned here, but only that he lives again by virtue of an act of God. The purpose of the statement goes beyond the regaining of life to the bestowal of position in the cosmos, in the universe, upon him who has been obedient. This is made clear by the bestowal of a name. A name is not a matter of chance, of no concern, but implies what is essential. A person is what he is called. This was how biblical man felt. We do not yet know what name is bestowed on Jesus. But the transcendent status of the existence signified by this name can be seen in the statement that God " highly " exalted him.

In the mythical overview an acclamation is now accorded to the exalted one. But who acclaims him? It is fairly clear that a phrase from the prophet Isaiah has been woven into the hymn: " To me every knee shall bow, every tongue shall swear "

(Is. 45:23b). In the prophecy it was the nations who were severely oppressing God's people Israel, and who at the end would acknowledge him and worship the one God, to their salvation. The nations are replaced in this hymn by those in heaven, on earth, and under the earth. Its scope is the whole cosmos. But it is not referring to men, but to *powers*. It is these powers which have hitherto enslaved man's destiny and reduced human existence to slavery. For them to bow the knee to Christ means not only that they recognize him as more powerful than they, but also that their rule is broken. A total *change of rule in the universe* has been inaugurated. Jesus, the obedient one, who is now highly exalted, has taken up the position of ruler of the universe.

This is expressly acknowledged by the powers when they say: "Jesus Christ is Lord." The emphasis in this confession lies on the word "Lord," and we learn from this what the name is that God bestowed upon him. The confession of Jesus as Lord, *kyrios,* is the oldest Christian confession of faith. "If you confess with your lips that Jesus is Lord and believe in your heart that God raised him from the dead, you will be saved" (Rom. 10:9). The only odd thing is that it is supra-terrestrial powers which utter this confession in the hymn, and not men, not the church. But there is no doubt that the church, from whose liturgy the hymn was taken, as we have heard, did not fail to participate, but made known its faith in Jesus as Lord in this way.

What is the theological and timeless meaning of the statement that the powers have had their powers taken from them? If the powers are the expression of the terror of human existence, in which man sees himself cast into the arms of a blind fate, then their dethronement symbolizes the bringing back of the world to God. The central significance of the world and of man is no longer found in meaninglessness, blindness, and chance, but in Jesus Christ. He is the answer to the questions which preoccupy men. In him the world is brought back to its meaning.

The dominion he holds is peace and salvation. The name "Lord," which is drawn here from an Old Testament quotation, is equivalent to the divine name of the Old Testament. From now on this Jesus Christ is God's openness to the world, the access, the mediator, the way. His dominion is not one of slavery and oppression, but of redemption and leading home.

Redemption and leading home have become possible in Christ Jesus. He has revealed obedience as a saving act. He who is in Christ Jesus, who is a Christian, comes under the claim of obedience and must be guided by obedience.

The saving action ends in the *glory of God the Father*. With the mention of God the Father the church is brought in, for although the powers know of God, they do not speak of the Father. But the church knows of the Father of its Lord Jesus Christ, and knows that through this Lord it has been given God as a Father. "For you did not receive the spirit of slavery to fall back into fear, but you have received the spirit of sonship [in which] we cry 'Abba! Father!'" (Rom. 8:15).

The Concern for Salvation (2:12–13)

12 Therefore, my beloved, as you have always obeyed, so now not only as in my presence but much more in my absence, work out your own salvation with fear and trembling; 13 for God is at work in you, both to will and to work for his good pleasure.

The word "obedience" is taken as a key word out of the hymn of Christ. Not only is there a mention of the obedience of the

Philippians hitherto but it is expected of them in the future. It is the apostle who calls for obedience. Paul has the right, the authority, and the duty to demand from his churches that they are obedient to him, and he has occasionally exerted his authority very firmly with the churches. He recalls the time when he was present in Philippi, when he first preached the gospel to them. Submission to the gospel is the *obedience of faith.* This they gave on that occasion. Now they should remain aware of their common responsibility for salvation.

Paul speaks of " your salvation." The church is an organized body, a number of men who are grouped together and ordered in relation to one another. They should edify each other, but they can also destroy each other. In their mutual concern for each other they are strong. We must note that " you " is plural, that the passage does not say that each must be concerned for his own salvation. Such a statement would actually be unchristian if it excluded a concern for the salvation of others. They must work out their salvation *in common.*

Human responsibility for one's fellow men is very sharply emphasized. It is almost as if everything depended on it. Then a statement follows which seems to be the exact opposite of what has just been said: that God works everything, both what is willed and what is brought about. Does Paul intend to contradict the first statement? Not at all. The paradox must remain. Everything depends on God and everything depends on man. But God is the initiator, the cause, the basis, the perfecter. One should not get the idea that God's action and man's can be separated, dissected, so that God continues where man leaves off, or that man has to collapse so that God can lift him up. God embraces Christian existence, the life of the church. He even incites the will, which is first stubborn and unnoticed, then active and urgent. Nor does he leave what he has begun, for it to continue on its own. God is faithful. He is moved and guided by graciousness and affection. His love is immeasurably great.

The Church in the World (2:14–18)

14*Do all things without grumbling or questioning,* 15*that you may be blameless and innocent, the children of God without blemish in the midst of a crooked and perverse generation, among whom you shine as lights in the world,* 16*holding fast the word of life, so that in the day of Christ I may be proud that I did not run in vain or labor in vain.* 17*Even if I am to be poured as a libation upon the sacrificial offering of your faith, I am glad and rejoice with you all.* 18*Likewise you also should be glad and rejoice with me.*

Paul likes to take up the images, types, and foreshadowings of the Old Testament, in order to describe and explain the church's situation to it. The people of God of the old covenant represent a foreshadowing. In their unbelief and because of their unreceptiveness to the gospel of Christ they were rejected, but the church should learn from their fate, their progress, and their errors. The generation of Moses in the desert and the wandering people of God in the forty years' journey to the promised land form in particular a type of foreshadowing of the new people of God. The murmuring against the men of God in the desert provoked Yahweh's anger. Since then murmuring has been characteristic of an improper attitude towards God. It is more than discontent with one's situation, or impatience, because underlying such an attitude is disobedience and the insidious signs of unbelief. Thus the warning " Do not grumble " is the counterpart and equivalent to the call to be obedient.

The church is set apart from the world. They are set apart as " saints " because they now belong to God. But they are not withdrawn from the world, and have no right to be. The tension and the test of Christianity lie in belonging to God and the world at the same time. Paul uses a phrase from Deuteronomy to draw a firm line between the church and the world: here are the children of God; there is a crooked and perverse generation (Deut. 32:5). This may well have been the way the earliest churches saw themselves, even though they were only insignificant groups in the middle of great cities, on which the apostle, with his practical sense of reality, concentrated. But this sense of being a diaspora, a number of small scattered groups of believers, did not bring with it the self-complacent awareness of being the chosen, a small exclusive sect. True grace does not bring pride, but humility, and alarm at the obligation that has been taken on. This obligation is not less than that the church should be the light of the world. If Christ is the innermost significance of the world, those who believe in him have the function of making manifest to the world the meaning he gives it.

They could never do this, even if they were transfigured. The illuminating power comes from the *word of life,* the gospel, which has been entrusted to the church. They can do no more than hold fast to this word, to be faithful to it, and profess it.

Faith must be endured to the end. It has an *aim*. Sometimes faith seems easy, when the church's shared experience is at its most intense, in the feeling of being among brethren, and in inspired enthusiasm. These moments have a lot to offer, but they are not decisive. It is the bringing to realization of faith in everyday life, perseverance, and loyalty which really matters.

The apostle, the pastor, is responsible for the church until the very end, until they come to the judgment seat of God. Then they will be his glory. But not all his trouble is rewarded. Sometimes he can run in vain. This is not resignation; it is only an expression of concern.

Paul makes quite clear the extent of the commitment he is ready and willing to undertake. He is prepared to go to the ultimate, to the sacrifice of his life. Once again he returns to the thought of death. He does not know whether he may yet be released from prison. But this time he sees his death in relation to the church. The church is seen as a great temple in which the service due to God is offered. Paul's joy at this moment is that their faith and service to God is so lively. No one could take this joy from him, even if his life were demanded, even if his blood was poured out like a libation. A fourfold sharing of joy closes that part of the epistle which consists of exhortation. He assures them that he rejoices with them, and wishes them to rejoice with him.

When the Philippians heard that their apostle Paul was in prison they may have been very worried about him. In their concern, how would they have received his letter of joy? Shocked, horrified, perplexed? Comforted, their minds set at rest, pleased? The apostle's purpose would have been satisfied if his testimony of faith had proved contagious.

TIMOTHY AND EPAPHRODITUS (2:19—3:1a)

In his letters to the churches Paul frequently gives information about what he plans to do in the immediate future. He does so here. But he has been deprived of his liberty, and has a very limited opportunity to make plans. Thus he must let others take his place and represent him to the church. Two men from his company now come into prominence, Timothy and Epaphroditus. The epistle once again takes on a personal note.

Timothy (2:19–24)

19*I hope in the Lord Jesus to send Timothy to you soon, so that I may be cheered by news of you.* 20*I have no one like him, who will be genuinely anxious for your welfare.* 21*They all look after their own interests, not those of Jesus Christ.* 22*But Timothy's worth you know, how as a son with a father he has served with me in the gospel.* 23*I hope therefore to send him just as soon as I see how it will go with me;* 24*and I trust in the Lord that shortly I myself shall come also.*

Timothy is to travel from Ephesus to Philippi. But at the present moment this is not possible. Therefore Paul says that he hopes to send him. And even this plan is placed in a religious context. The hope is "in the Lord Jesus." Timothy is to find out what has been happening to the Philippians in the meantime, and to report it to Paul. The announcement of this journey by his colleague contains a hidden impulse which says much for the noble and warmhearted nature of Paul's relationship with this particular church. He is confident about them, and expects to hear nothing from them except good news which will cheer him.

A note of discord is now heard. Paul looks round his colleagues and feels bound to pass a harsh judgment on them. It concerns those who are at his disposal at present, or who could be available. They may not have been many. Perhaps something had happened which he does not mention, but which may be connected with his imprisonment. Had he become isolated? His outward distress is deepened by an inner one.

The judgment he makes takes its standard from the conviction on which it passes judgment. This must be carefully noted. This is what makes it a true Christian judgment. A colleague of the apostle has to be concerned for the good of the church. This is identical with the cause of Christ. Anyone who instead thinks of himself has things the wrong way around. Paul is certainly not concerned to unmask or blame anyone among his immediate colleagues. He names no names. But once again he does not hesitate to call evil by its name. It may have been no easy task to serve with Paul. But his colleagues possessed a valid standard by which to measure themselves, the example of Paul and his critical, incisive words, which he did not hold back.

But he prefers to give praise, and here he praises Timothy. The testimony given to him here is unique in the whole New Testament. He excels the others, and once again it is the nature of his personal conviction which matters. It is now obvious why Paul includes him with himself in the opening words of the letter. He too is a slave of Jesus Christ. He too serves the gospel. There is a considerable age gap between them, so that Paul can call him his child. But this does not detract from the appreciation of him which he expresses to the church. He is not unknown to the Philippians. They know his worth from their own experience. When missionary work was first carried out in their city, they had the opportunity to see how committed he was.

After this really solemn introduction Paul reaffirms his plan. " I hope therefore to send him . . ." There is therefore sufficient reason already for them to give him a worthy reception. But he will not come until Paul's case has been decided before the court. It is clear that this will not be long. The judge's decision can be expected in the immediate future. Paul's hope of seeing the Philippians again soon breaks through. His trust in the Lord is firm.

Epaphroditus (2:25—3:1a)

25I have thought it necessary to send to you Epaphroditus my
brother and fellow worker and fellow soldier, and your messenger
and minister to my need, 26for he has been longing for you all,
and has been distressed because you heard that he was ill.
27Indeed he was ill, near to death. But God had mercy on him,
and not only on him but on me also, lest I should have sorrow
upon sorrow. 28I am the more eager to send him, therefore, that
you may rejoice at seeing him again, and that I may be less
anxious. 29So receive him in the Lord with all joy; and honor
such men, for he nearly died for the work of Christ, risking his
life to complete your service to me. 1aFinally, my brethren,
rejoice in the Lord.

Paul's second close companion is Epaphroditus. He was not Paul's colleague on his mission, but a member, perhaps a leading member, of the church at Philippi. The Philippians had sent him to Paul in prison, to bring him their alms and probably also to remain with him. They wanted to know that there was someone close to him of whom he was fond and who would be at his disposal if he needed help. The significance of this action says much for the Philippians. They knew and felt that financial or material gifts alone are not sufficient, and can perhaps even wound, if they are not evidence of personal inclination, attachment, and respect.

Epaphroditus' mission was not an easy one. It needed courage to go to someone who was imprisoned, and whose "offense" was moreover a very vague one. It is no wonder that Paul was very grateful to him.

But now he sends him back, earlier than had been expected. The reason is that Epaphroditus had fallen ill, although he had now recovered. Besides his illness, he longed to return, and the two things were connected. There is no reason to reproach him for this. Some in Philippi seem to have done so. Paul takes his helper completely under his protection. The almost fatal illness from which he had suffered had naturally been of serious concern to Paul as well, and this was another factor. That he was saved from death is attributed to God's mercy. For Paul God is not a remote figure, far away from the life and misery of men. He sees God as planning and disposing, helping, saving and judging. And therefore he knows that when Epaphroditus was saved he himself was helped. And this again brings him joy.

But Epaphroditus is given back to the church as a fine example of the service of Christ. To take on and carry responsibility shows excellence and must be recognized. This is right and proper, and Paul wishes it to be so regarded in his churches. There are only a few who are able and willing to take on a special function. The outward success of a mission is not what really matters. A mission can fail through external circumstances, like that of Epaphroditus, who was not really expected back yet in Philippi. And yet all the Philippians are in his debt. It is astonishing how Paul is able to put things right. Epaphroditus has added human feeling to the church's gift. Without him the gift would have lacked something. And he risked his life to provide this.

There is once again a call to joy, the note that runs through the whole epistle.

A WARNING AGAINST FALSE DOCTRINES (3:1b—4:1)

At this point in the epistle it turns to a fresh subject. We hear of false doctrines, of those who disturb the peace, of opponents who have penetrated the church from outside. The unity and faith of Christianity in Philippi is threatened. Paul makes a sharp attack on these people. It is difficult to say exactly where they came from and what their true aims and intentions were. The motive for their action seems to have been an exuberant and enthusiastic doctrine of perfection. They imagined that they had achieved perfection, or were at least safely on the way to it, so that they were convinced that they had no farther to go. But salvation is never a possession, at one's disposal. Paul makes this emphatically clear.

Because the situation of the church at Philippi which is assumed here seems to be different from that in the first two chapters of the epistle, a number of scholars have argued that chapter 3 is a separate epistle to the Philippians by Paul, which he sent later and which was edited into one epistle by combining it with the first at a later stage. There is no need to go into this matter here. It is sufficient for us to remember that this part of the epistle forms a separate whole in itself.

Do Not Be Led Astray (3:1b–6)

1b*To write the same things to you is not irksome to me, and is*

safe for you. 2*Look out for the dogs, look out for the evil-*
workers, look out for those who mutilate the flesh. 3*For we are*
the true circumcision, who worship God in spirit, and glory in
Christ Jesus, and put no confidence in the flesh. 4*Though I*
myself have reason for confidence in the flesh also. If any other
man thinks he has reason for confidence in the flesh, I have
more : 5*circumcised on the eighth day, of the people of Israel, of*
the tribe of Benjamin, a Hebrew born of Hebrews; as to the law
a Pharisee, 6*as to zeal a persecutor of the church, as to righteous-*
ness under the law blameless.

In almost all his churches, in Corinth, in Galatia, and now in Philippi as well, Paul had to fight against false missionaries who followed in his tracks and preached a gospel different from his. For the churches this brought threat and uncertainty, while for Paul it was a danger to his own life's work. He did everything in his power to preserve the true faith of Christ, the true gospel. It is difficult to say whether in his lifetime he succeeded in this. But at a later period his apostolic authority was established, and his gospel with it. This confirms what has ever since been the experience of the church, that upheavals, crises, and convulsions are necessary if the gospel is to be accepted, affirmed, and spread in its true form. The transition of the gospel from the Jewish world of Syria and Palestine into the Greek world brought together two different cultures and modes of life. Conflicts were inevitable.

Paul is only rarely sarcastic. He calls the people concerned " dogs," evilworkers and mutilators. The term " dog " was then, as it is today, a term of abuse. In the Jewish sphere it was frequently applied to apostates, heretics, and unbelievers. This is the intention here. Their dedication, their efforts, their missionary work are futile, harmful, and destructive. By mutilation Paul is hinting at the Jewish practices in which they gloried, and to circumcision in particular, which they propagated, or at least valued as a sign of salvation.

For Paul the Old Testament people of God had been superseded. If anyone asked where the old ordinance remained, or who had inherited the old covenant, Paul said: " We are the circumcision." The really important factor, which is decisive here, is the Spirit, who has become effective through Christ Jesus. The Spirit has made possible a new service, carried out in Christ. The Spirit is the opposite of the flesh. The flesh refers to the world, and in particular the world in its self-assertiveness, the attempt to find autonomy and salvation in itself. But this throws man back on his own resources, and shows the dubious nature of his confidence. Confidence and glorying go together. They give security, or at least try to persuade one that it is there. There is a false and a true confidence and glorying; both are justified only in Christ Jesus.

Paul begins to compare himself with his opponents. The battleground is clearly defined. The purpose of the dispute is not to show that he is more qualified by reason of his religious practice than his opponents. Rather, the Philippians are meant to learn from the example of their apostle to make the right decision for themselves in the face of the danger that threatens them. For what his opponents valued as religious privileges, Paul can also claim for himself. This is the first thing he has to point out to them. He looks back to the past, and Paul's past is that of a Jew. He grew up in an orthodox Jewish home, where he was circumcised, in accordance with the law, on the eighth day after his birth. His home was in the diaspora, the scattered colonies of Jews away from Palestine, and was in fact in Tarsus in Cilicia.

But it could not be taken for granted that a Jew would live faithfully in accordance with the traditional faith and the customs of his fathers. The title " Hebrew " accorded to both him and his parents certifies that they had remained faithful to Judaism. For in the diaspora it distinguished in particular those Jews who practiced the customs of the Judaism of their homeland in Palestine, and used Hebrew as their mother tongue. King Saul also belonged to the tribe of Benjamin and it was his name which the apostle was given by his parents.

What his parents had tried to arouse and nourish in him was continued, intensified, and made more radical by him as he grew up. He became a Pharisee, and so joined the religious party in Judaism which was based on a rigorous application of the law. He clearly recognized that Christianity of its nature contained within itself in embryo form the power to overcome Judaism, and he energetically opposed the first development within Judaism. Paul is not happy in describing this period of his life, and he must sometimes have been reproached for it in the church. But he leaves no doubt that his Judaism in the past was sincere and honest, and that he is qualified and competent to speak as he does about the distinction between Judaism and Christianity.

The Change in the Apostle's Life (3:7–11)

[7]But whatever gain I had, I counted as loss for the sake of Christ. [8]Indeed I count everything as loss because of the surpassing worth of knowing Christ Jesus my Lord. For his sake I have suffered the loss of all things, and count them as refuse, in order that I may gain Christ [9]and be found in him, not having a righteousness of my own, based on law, but that which is through

faith in Christ, the righteousness from God that depends on faith; 10*that I may know him and the power of his resurrection, and may share his sufferings, becoming like him in his death,* 11*that if possible I may attain the resurrection from the dead.*

His previous life as a Jew had been sincere. There can be no doubt about this. But now his life has taken a different course. The change is marked by a single phrase, "for the sake of Christ." This phrase is important. The hope of Judaism was for the Messiah who was to come. In him the promise of Israel's full redemption would be fulfilled. As a Jew, Paul had shared this hope. But he recognized that the promise had already become a reality in Jesus, who was confessed by the Christian church which he was persecuting. The title "Christ" carries its full meaning here, and has not yet hardened into a proper name. Of course, the reality was different from the expectation. Israel was excluded from faith in Christ, and the majority of Jews had rejected the gospel. The new people of God was composed of Gentiles. Paul, the former Jew, felt deep pain at the path taken by Israel: "I am speaking the truth in Christ, I am not lying . . . that I have great sorrow and unceasing anguish in my heart. For I could wish that I myself were accursed and cut off from Christ for the sake of my brethren, my kinsmen by race. They are Israelites . . ." (Rom. 9:1–4).

The change took place for Paul in his experience at Damascus. There is no doubt that here he is looking back on that event. It was an act of grace. He was overpowered by Christ. But he speaks as if it had been his decision, which he even clothes in the commercial language of gain and loss, as though he had calculated it. In the face of the threat to the Philippians, he is concerned to show the church by his example the decision and the way which alone can lead to Christ. Half-measures and compromises are not discussed. They would be a betrayal.

Even though the beginning of Paul's path as a Christian was an absolute act of grace, he was not absolved from the decision, the resolution, the act of acceptance. The act of grace is meant to exercise a continuing effect, to be prolonged in human life. Thus cooperation is necessary. The beginning that has been made must be sustained, taken over, brought to realization. Paul gave his acceptance, and affirms it ever more strongly. What he regarded as a loss he still sees as a loss, and even as refuse, filth, dung.

There are passages in his epistles which are simply a riddle to us. How is it possible for someone to pass judgment in such words on his own past, and on everything that had meant anything to him and was of any profit, on the revered tradition and sacred heritage of his fathers? He will not have any compromise. This is the moment when Christianity parts company with Judaism. He must have needed this rigorism, in order to draw the dividing line clearly. Only one thing is now worth anything: the surpassing worth of knowing Christ Jesus. The men of the Bible did not feel that knowledge was something purely theoretical, an intellectual process, an approval granted by the understanding. It always embraced and comprehended all man's powers, and was personal. Thus Paul can speak of the knowledge of *his* Lord. It was this personal, total existential knowledge which he was given at Damascus.

He drew the consequences. He gave up everything that meant anything to him, and from then on was moved only by the desire to gain Christ. This desire can only be fulfilled on the last day which is to come. Only then will it be seen whether or not anyone will truly be found in Christ, and is or has been a Christian.

In Paul's writings, the antithesis of law and faith plays a dominant role in the separation and conflict between Christianity and Judaism. Is it the law or faith which leads to salvation? In theological terms, the choice can be expressed as the question: Do I become righteous before God by the law or by faith? The issue he touches on here is discussed at length in Romans and Galatians (cf. Rom. 1—8; Gal. 2:15—5:26). Paul nevertheless recalls it in his argument against the heresy in Philippi.

The law and the observance of the law lead to a righteousness that is man's own creation. In confronting God man relies on his "own" righteousness. But Paul sees in this man's original sin, that he separates himself from God, falls back on his own resources, and believes that he can hold his own, justify himself, and prove himself. The role of the law, with all its meticulousness and ambivalence, but also its divinely willed purposefulness, is recognized. Paul summarily deprives man of the law as a means of self-assertion before God, by pointing out that the only righteousness which is from God is that which comes *through faith* in Christ. The other is egotistical; it is self-righteousness. Righteousness, saving action, can come only from God, and is a gift of grace in an exclusive sense. Man's urge towards self-assertion must be destroyed. Only when man sees that he is wholly dependent on grace is he able to have faith.

Knowledge of Christ, as a personal knowledge, is concerned in the first instance with his suffering, his death, and his resurrection. It includes a readiness to accept privations, suffering, and shame, particularly when they are endured for the sake of faith, in the imitation of Christ. Then the Christian becomes like his Christ. He is meant for this from his baptism. "Do you not know that all of us who have been baptized into Christ Jesus were baptized into his death?" (Rom. 6:3). The law of the believer's life is to be conformed to Christ in a continuous process, to become like Christ. In this process he can experience the life-giving power of the risen Lord as a transforming force: the forgiveness of sins, the gifts of grace, the redemption from deadly peril.

In this matter the opponents seem to have held a different opinion. The suffering figure of the apostle seems to have been an offense to them. They refused to share suffering, but accepted the power of the resurrection. They believed that in their one-sided view they were safe. For them, the future new life had not merely begun already—Paul was in agreement with them about this—but was already there in its fullness.

Not Yet Perfected (3:12–16)

12*Not that I have already obtained this or am already perfect;*
but I press on to make it my own, because Christ Jesus has made
me his own. 13*Brethren, I do not consider that I have made it*
my own; but one thing I do, forgetting what lies behind and
straining forward to what lies ahead, 14*I press on towards the*
goal for the prize of the upward call of God in Christ Jesus. 15*Let*
those of us who are mature be thus minded; and if in anything
you are otherwise minded, God will reveal that also to you.
16*Only let us hold true to what we have attained.*

Paul disassociates himself completely from this false view. He is not yet perfect, and has not yet obtained the resurrection. He sees himself as on a journey in which he has to devote all his powers to drawing nearer to his goal. One can scarcely imagine a Christian who dedicated himself more actively, more joyfully, and more sacrificially to his purpose than Paul. He too, of course, had to work, to practice renunciation, to be patient, to learn. But what might seem from outside to be a hectic bustle was inwardly nourished from other sources. Christ had taken hold of him and set him on the right path. He whom he sought to obtain had already made him his own.

It is foolishness to think that one has already obtained him. A belief in one's perfection brings with it the danger of letting the moral will grow slack. The image of the runner in a race, so widespread at the time, explains the situation (cf. 1 Cor. 9: 24–27). There is a prize to be won, but it can also be lost. A runner in the stadium does not think of the distance he has already covered, still less does he imagine the prize already won, and dream of himself in the ecstasy of victory. It is too easy to be overtaken. The laurel has still to be won. This is God's call to his heavenly kingdom.

Those who imagine they are perfect should remember this. The nature of Christian existence as a pilgrimage is precarious. As a pilgrim (*homo viator*), the Christian gives the lie to all the false claims that perfection can be found within this world, and that the human spirit can reach out to take hold of the rewards of the last day. His task is not easy, for it is unpopular, and reminds men that the world is frail.

Revelations and ecstasies may also have played a not unimportant role among Paul's opponents. Paul refers ironically to this. When religion turns away from the truth, remarkable oddities and pseudo-religious happenings become prominent. Paul is wise enough to recognize what is necessary: not to yield, not to fall back from what has been attained, and to carry on along the way on which we have set out.

The Last Day Brings Perfection (3:17—4:1)

[17]*Brethren, join in imitating me, and mark those who so live as*
you have an example in us. [18]*For many, of whom I have often*
told you and now tell you even with tears, live as enemies of the
cross of Christ. [19]*Their end is destruction, their god is the belly,*
and they glory in their shame, with minds set on earthly things.
[20]*But our commonwealth is in heaven, and from it we await a*
Saviour, the Lord Jesus Christ, [21]*who will change our lowly body*
to be like his glorious body, by the power which enables him
even to subject all things to himself. [1]*Therefore, my brethren,*
whom I love and long for, my joy and crown, stand firm thus
in the Lord, my beloved.

Paul's warnings still require to be supplemented by positive guidance, by a straightforward rule which points the way forward. The solution he offers is a simple one, yet at the same time a difficult one: Paul offers himself for *imitation*. The idea of the imitation of Paul occurs frequently in his epistles, and indeed was the underlying idea at the beginning of the chapter, where the Philippians were asked to learn from his resolves and decisions in the past.

The imitation of Paul is developed in two directions. In the first place Paul is an example not because of himself, for he is only the mediator of the example of Christ. His statements must be expounded in the sense of 1 Corinthians 11:1: "Be imitators of me, as I am of Christ." Here the mediating position which Paul occupies, as pastor, between Christ and the church is made clear. The example offered, the pattern, is necessarily a supplement to the word that is preached. They enrich each other.

An open and ready heart is also necessary to understand and accept the pattern given without words.

The other development brings in his colleagues and the churches. All who have resolved to accept the preaching of Christ and the pattern given by Paul are now in a position, and called, to be an example to others. This is mutual edification. Believers are brought into relationship with one another in a very definite way.

But it is possible to give not only an edifying example but a destructive one. Paul can speak only with tears of those who do so. The enemies of the cross of Christ are not merely to be sought among the unbelievers, those who reject the gospel. They are also widespread among the faithful themselves and are at work spreading their dangerous propaganda. They include those who are teaching false doctrine at Philippi. We now learn what is the root of their error: the scandal of the cross. They deny the cross, just as they draw back from suffering and privation in their own lives. The two attitudes form a unity. They worship the glorified Christ and indulge their belief in their own perfection.

But to pass by the cross is to miss the heart of Paul's gospel, and to become an apostate. Paul can only foretell their *judgment,* their destruction. Using words that derive from a general polemic against heretics, he describes what his opponents are like. What they consider praiseworthy is shameful; their mind is wholly set on earthly things.

The home of the Christian church is "in heaven." Paul sets the members of the church on this plane not in order to free them from earthly responsibility, but to make them aware that they are strangers here, and that heaven and earth cannot be exchanged for each other, as his opponents are trying to do.

The step forward to perfection has still to be taken. Not until the Lord Jesus appears from heaven will perfection be attained. In this context we find the word *soter,* "Saviour."

We know that in the Greek and Roman world the expression "saviour" was a common one. But there is no reference here to a saviour cult, such as that of the emperor. The function of the *kyrios,* the heavenly Lord, as a saviour, is concentrated upon the end, upon the final act with which he will bring redemption to completion.

In this life "our lowly body" sometimes, or perhaps constantly, reminds us that the development of the potentials of human life is very limited, and that redemption is still to come. Earthly existence is bodily existence. This does not mean that corporeal, bodily existence will once and for all be replaced by an existence which is one of the soul, and is therefore not bodily. Paul does not think in the categories of Hellenistic anthropology, which clearly distinguished soul and body. Even if he was acquainted with it, another point of view is more important and more essential for him: that of conformity to Christ, which is ensured by faith. This is brought to completion by the transformation of our bodily existence, and indeed of the whole of our existence. The lowly body will be transformed into the image of his glorious body. The image of Christ receives its full expression when man participates in the glory of his resurrection.

This is what faith hopes for. It is based on the power and omnipotence that is accorded to the Lord, the *kyrios*. But it is a power for salvation. We should not tremble before it, but cling to it. Christian life is aimed at redemption. It is in tension between one salvation and another, the one given to us in the sign of the cross, which lays down the law for our earthly life, and the other which will bring us to perfection. Both are linked to the name of Christ Jesus.

Between these two moments we have to stand firm in the Lord. The temptations and blows are many. The Philippians, who are Paul's joy, will one day be his crown, in the day of Christ. The bond between the church and its apostle endures beyond the bounds of time.

CONCLUDING REQUESTS AND DISCUSSION (4:2–20)

The concluding chapter brings together a series of separate matters: a request to a leader of the church to take care of two women; exhortations, once again to the whole church; and finally Paul's thanks for the support he has been given, expressed in uniquely beautiful words.

Euodia and Syntyche (4:2–3)

2*I entreat Euodia and I entreat Syntyche to agree in the Lord.*
3*And I ask you also, true yokefellow, help these women, for they have labored side by side with me in the gospel together with Clement and the rest of my fellow workers, whose names are in the book of life.*

Paul turns to completely concrete matters. He has been told that in Philippi there are two women who have quarrelled. Because they must have played a particularly important role in social and church life, their quarrel is doing great harm to the church. They are called back to harmony and concord, and this exhortation should be seen in connection with the instruction given as the beginning of chapter 2. It is not often that we are given in one of Paul's epistles so direct an insight into the life of the church. Paul knew the two women Euodia and Syntyche personally. One must not imagine that the earliest congregations were groups of ideal human beings. Like every church, they were threatened by sin. Brotherly reproof and a readiness to accept it is the way to restore good order.

A certain Syzygos (" yokefellow ") who has shown himself a true colleague of Paul's, and presumably carried out some leading function at Philippi, is asked to make things up between the women. We learn that they were there when the church was being founded and gave great help to the missionaries. There is also someone called Clement and numerous others who were among the first Christians in Philippi. God had chosen them. Their names were known to him from the first.

Joy, Peace, and Perseverance (4:4–9)

4*Rejoice in the Lord always; again I will say, Rejoice.* 5*Let all men know your forbearance. The Lord is at hand.* 6*Have no anxiety about anything, but in everything by prayer and supplication with thanksgiving let your requests be made known to God.* 7*And the peace of God, which passes all understanding, will keep your hearts and your minds in Christ Jesus.* 8*Finally, brethren, whatever is true, whatever is honorable, whatever is just, whatever is pure, whatever is lovely, whatever is gracious, if there is any excellence, if there is anything worthy of praise, think about these things.* 9*What you have learned and received and heard and seen in me, do; and the God of peace will be with you.*

Paul's thought turns once again to joy. It now becomes quite clear that this joy is something that lies beyond natural experience, and also that it must be a basic condition of Christian life; for they are called to rejoice always. The inner emotion and vitality come to the surface. Joy in the Lord is a sign of the kindness and gentleness which should shine out from the church upon the world around. The church should be a light in the world.

How much lack of understanding, hatred, and meanness there is, and how difficult it is for love, understanding, and gentleness to prevail against them. If they are places of mutual love, Christian churches can exercise a power of attraction and act as a focus. The lack of love makes them dim and flickering. One source of their joy is that the Lord is near. The prayers of the early church used to close with the cry: Maranatha, come, O Lord! We too can say the same, even if we are no longer filled with the imminent hope of the end of all things. It is possible, reasonable, and desirable for us to look forward to the coming of the Lord, because we have a future, and he is our future.

A prayer of blessing calls down the peace of God upon the church. Peace is salvation. If it comes from God, it surpasses human dimensions and comprehension. The danger to faith is always acute. Unbelief tries to establish itself even in the believer. The heart produces doubts, questions that can lead to murmuring, especially when earthly existence is threatened, and even more in the *peirasmos*, the time of trial. God's protection is necessary. It has the power to preserve us, and is vouchsafed in the realm of Christ Jesus.

In the realm which is outside Christ there is no doubt that virtue, honor, love, and heroism can be found. It would be presumptuous and deceitful to restrict them to the realm of Christianity. Paul knew of the good in the world. He was not afraid to repeat for the guidance of his churches the ethical texts, moral concepts, and lists of virtues of the surrounding world, of their heathen neighbors. At that time there were many wandering philosopher-preachers, stoics or cynics in their outlook, who taught rules of life. Paul does not ignore them. When he encourages truthfulness, honorableness, justice, purity, a stoic could have said the same.

The least that follows from this is that the Christian church should never fall behind its neighbors in the standard of life it displays. If it did, it would be bearing a bad witness to itself. But what distinguishes it from its neighbors is the standard of faith. It has been given this by the apostle, both in his words and in his example. Since then its members have studied in the school of Christianity, and learned their faith. Traditions are beginning to grow up, and they can be handed on.

Thus the church in the diaspora, as a small group in a non-Christian environment, forms an area which is set apart from the world in a way that can only be understood by faith. There is no difference between the people in it and those near it. There is virtue to be found among both. But faith is on the side of the church, and faith is decisive. And it is faith that has the promise of the peace of God.

The Apostle's Thanksgiving (4:10–20)

[10]*I rejoice in the Lord greatly that now at length you have*
revived your concern for me; you were indeed concerned for
me, but you had no opportunity. [11]*Not that I complain of want;*
for I have learned, in whatever state I am, to be content. [12]*I know*
how to be abased, and I know how to abound; in any and all
circumstances I have learned the secret of facing plenty and
hunger, abundance and want. [13]*I can do all things in him who*
strengthens me. [14]*Yet it was kind of you to share my trouble.*

15 *And you Philippians yourselves know that in the beginning of*
the gospel, when I left Macedonia, no church entered into
partnership with me in giving and receiving except you only;
16 *for even in Thessalonica you sent me help once and again.* 17 *Not*
that I seek the gift; but I seek the fruit which increases to your
credit. 18 *I have received full payment, and more; I am filled,*
having received from Epaphroditus the gifts you sent, a fragrant
offering, a sacrifice acceptable and pleasing to God. 19 *And my*
God will supply every need of yours according to his riches in
glory in Christ Jesus. 20 *To our God and Father be glory forever*
and ever. Amen.

Paul once again turns to personal matters. He now expresses his thanks for the gift which the Philippians had sent him with Epaphroditus. One would have expected these thanks to be uttered earlier in the epistle, but the urgent concern of the church, and of Paul himself, has been put first. He is not writing a private letter, but is writing to carry out his apostolic task. This explains the form his thanks take. It seems very odd.

The first impression it gives is that he had been impatient that the support from the Philippians had been a long time in coming. That they were finally able to exercise their concern for him again is a cause for joy. But Paul is almost wholly unconcerned about his own person. He is as objective as can be. He puts himself completely in their place, judges entirely from their point of view, and so shares their joy, which consisted in finding an opportunity for helping him after having looked for one for a long time. Thus he defends them; their good will, which was always present, is recognized.

Every misunderstanding must be excluded. His words are not dictated by his necessity. There is no mention of his suffering, even though he is in prison. His apostolic calling had subjected him to a hard school, and he describes elsewhere the discipline of suffering he had undergone. It extends from flogging, danger from robbers, hunger, and thirst to stoning and even to shipwreck at sea (cf. 2 Cor. 6:3–10; 11:23–33). He can tolerate all this.

Discipline must be exercised in both poverty and abundance. The overcoming of poverty and want is certainly the hardest. And Paul exaggerates a little when he speaks of himself as having abundance. The wanderer, always on the move, has no opportunity to store up provisions. All he means to say is that he also knows the temptation of plenty. And this too he has learned to overcome.

Is Paul such an ascetic? Has he such a masterful control over himself? It is clear that he was impulsive, full of vitality, and strong-willed. But his true power comes from elsewhere. There is one who makes him strong, and that is Christ. Indeed, he knows that his weakness is the means Christ uses to reveal his power.

From the very first he had a good relationship of trust with the Philippians. Only a few weeks after he had left their city they began to provide him with the necessities of life. This they continued. Paul accepted this service. This was a mark of distinction for the Philippians, for he accepted support from only a few churches. He knew that the laborer is worthy of his hire, that the missionary and pastor have a right to be maintained by the churches, but he did not use this right, so that the gospel might not be hindered, and so that he should not be reproached. Philippi was a great exception. They could be proud of this.

Paul is not concerned with material gain, but with the

spiritual fruit. He values the gift as evidence of their good will, their sacrificial spirit, and therefore as a sign of their progress in the practice of the Christian life. To let someone share in one's own goods for the sake of the gospel demands a right frame of mind towards the word on the part of both the giver and the receiver.

Although Paul acknowledges their contribution, like the tradesman signing a receipt, there is something even more important for him underlying the gift. Man is served, but the human service is also a service to God. It is astonishing that Paul can describe the Philippians' gift as a sacrifice offered to God. "A sacrifice acceptable and pleasing to God" is an expression familiar to us from the cultic theology of the Old Testament (cf. Ex. 29:18; Ezek. 20:41). True sacrifices are spiritual. What counts before God is not the fat of goats and bullocks, but the love proclaimed in the service men do for each other, a love that stems from faith.

It is God who gives good gifts. To refer to God in such a context can easily seem to be a stumbling block to belief. But God with his riches is not thought of as filling gaps, as stepping into the breach made by human parsimony. God supplies *all* human need, both that of Paul and that of the Philippians. Before God, all human life is necessarily dependent.

The believer is called to share in the fullness of God's glory. This is to come in the future at the end of the ages. God gives himself, and gives a share in what is his own, particularly to those who are themselves ready to hand on what is theirs.

The conclusion is formed by a short prayer of praise. Paul closes the letter, as he began, with prayer.

THE CLOSE OF THE LETTER
(4:21-23)

CONCLUSION
(4:21–23)

[21]*Greet every saint in Christ Jesus. The brethren who are with me greet you.* [22]*All the saints greet you, especially those of Caesar's household.* [23]*The grace of the Lord Jesus Christ be with your spirit.*

An epistle usually ends with greetings, and the same is true today. But here we can see again that Paul's epistles are something out of the ordinary, the expression of his apostolic office, and also of the fraternal feeling that linked the churches together. The saints of Ephesus greet the saints of Philippi. They are fond of each other, not because of ties of blood, personal acquaintanceship, or affection, but because of the faith they share. This gives a consciousness of solidarity, of intentions for and shared with the brethren.

One group in the church of Ephesus is mentioned in particular, those of Caesar's household. These are imperial slaves, who may have served in the praetorium, where the court was held, so that Paul had the occasion to see them and speak to them. Some of them are Christians.

Both the church of Ephesus and that of Philippi have been founded by Paul. Thus his person also unites them. He adds to the greetings of the saints those of the brethren, his colleagues, who have access to him, and precedes them with his own. He greets every one of them, "every saint in Christ Jesus." This is a final testimony to the good relationship between him and the Philippians.

The blessing is the last thing he has to give. Epistles were read out when the church was assembled. The blessing sees them all as united in the spirit. One spirit inspires the whole church. This is an expression, testimony, and visible manifestation of the Spirit of God, who has created Christian life and the Christian church, and made them possible.

The Epistle to the Colossians

INTRODUCTION

"The mystery of Christ" (Col. 4:3) is really the mystery of Christianity. It was in order to remind the Christians at Colossae of this that St. Paul addressed this letter to the community there. There were urgent reasons for doing so; various opinions had arisen among them which threatened to obscure the mystery of Christ. There were heretics who demanded that Christians should venerate the "elements of the world" (2:8, 20) and this was combined with a curious "worship of the angels" (2:18) and the observance of all kinds of prescriptions concerning different times and types of food (2:16f.). The result was a complex mixture of Christian, Jewish, and pagan elements which turned faith into superstition. This was possible because the Colossians did not yet understand the mystery of Christ sufficiently. Consequently, St. Paul is at pains to explain it to them, as far as that is possible in a letter.

The gospel which had been preached to the Colossians by their fellow countryman Epaphras (1:5–7) could be summed up briefly as follows: Jesus Christ is the Lord of all creation and the only Saviour of the world. As a result of the activities of the heretics, however, Christ's unique position in creation and in the redemption was being called into doubt.

a) *Jesus Christ is the Lord of all creation*. Everything was created in him, through him, and for him; in him all subsist (1:16f.). He is the Head to which all the dominions and powers are subject (2:10). Therefore, there is no need to pay a special cult to the "elements of the world," apart from that which is paid to Christ; there is no need to speculate about mysterious divine powers which are concealed within creation. Christ who has been raised to glory has complete control over all such things; the whole plentitude of deity dwells in him (2:9). For a Christian, the world is stripped of its divine and magical character. It is something created, something which exists only for the glory of its Creator and the service of human beings. A Christian, therefore, never confuses the creature with the Creator. This enables him to be of real service to creation, in an appropriate manner.

b) *Jesus Christ is the only Saviour of the world*. It is he alone who reconciles the world with God; through his blood he has established peace, that peace which was promised for the last stage of time (1:20). He is "the first born of the dead" (1:18), and so he is the founder of the new humanity which is born of the waters of baptism (2:12f.). As a result of being raised from the dead, he enjoys the fullness of divine life and power. Consequently, all those who are raised with him in baptism are also "filled" (2:9) with his divine life; they already share in that salvation which overcomes death. Therefore they have no need to watch for any other alleged saviours the heretics may have to offer. The gospel proclaims to the whole world that the Saviour who was promised for the last stage of time is already among them; he is "in" them; in him they already share in the hope of glory to come (1:27). So by God's design, Christ has become the meaning and the goal of all history.

However, the salvation Christ brings does not fall into a person's lap. Neither is it to be obtained by the curious practices recommended by the heretics. Dying with Christ in baptism (2:11f.) demands that a person should live in him (2:6). This means putting off the old self and being clothed in the new self

(3:9f.); it means letting Christ act as the Lord who governs all the decisions which affect our lives (2:6), no matter what walk of life we are in (3:11, 18; 4:1). Our spiritual outlook must be changed, so that our thoughts are fixed " above " where Christ sits at the right hand of the Father (3:1f.) In this way, the " mystery of Christ " of which St. Paul speaks so eloquently in this epistle must bear fruit in our everyday lives. So shall we become " perfect human beings " (1:28) such as he will be glad to present to Christ at the judgment to come. It is only at the second coming of Christ that the " mystery of Christ " who is already our life, but in a hidden manner, will come into the open; then the glory of this mystery will be revealed in all its brilliance (3:4). This was what Christians hoped for in St. Paul's time and this is what they still hope for today; nothing must shift them away from it (1:23).

OUTLINE

The Opening of the Letter (1:1–2)

INTRODUCTORY VERSES (1 : 1–2)

I. The sender (1 : 1)

II. The addressees (1 : 2a)

III. Greetings (1 : 2b)

The Body of the Letter (1:3—4:6)

THE MYSTERY OF CHRIST (1 : 3—2 : 23)

I. St. Paul's thanksgiving for the community (1 : 3–8)

II. The object of his prayer; deeper insight into the salvation which is accorded them, and joyful gratitude for it (1 : 9–13)

III. A "Christological hymn" (1 : 14–20)

1. Redemption through Christ (1 : 14)
2. Christ the true likeness of the invisible God, the first-born of all creation (1 : 15)
3. Creation in Christ (1 : 16)
4. Christ takes precedence over all (1 : 17)
5. The Head of this body, the firstborn of the dead (1 : 18)
6. Christ possesses God's "fullness" (1 : 19)
7. All-encompassing reconciliation through him (1 : 20)

IV. The Colossians are reconciled through Christ (1 : 21–23)

V. St. Paul proclaims and executes God's "secret" (1:24–28)

1. St. Paul's happiness in his suffering for the church (1:24)
2. St. Paul's preaching as the revelation of a "secret" (1:25–26)
3. The secret: "Christ in you" (1:27)
4. The essence of St. Paul's exhortation: "promoting Christ" (1:28)

VI. St. Paul's struggle on behalf of the community (1:29—2:7)

1. His anxious "striving" (1:29—2:1)
2. That the communities may have a fuller understanding of Christ's secret (2:2–3)
3. That the community may be preserved from heretics (2:4–5)
4. An exhortation to live in Christ according to the tradition (2:6–7)

VII. A first warning against heresy (2:8)

VIII. Salvation and redemption through Christ alone (2:9–15)

1. Christ, the plenitude of Deity (2:9)
2. "Completed" in him (2:10)
3. "Circumcised" in him (2:11)
4. United with his burial and resurrection (2:12–13)
5. God cancelled the deed which excluded us, through Christ (2:14)
6. He disarmed the powers through him (2:15)

IX. A second warning against heresy with more precise references to its teachings (2:16–23)

1. Their superstitious practices (2:16–17)
2. The "mystery" character of the heresy (2:18)
3. Separation from the "Head" (2:19)
4. A warning against their "prescriptions" (2:20–21)
5. These are only human prescriptions (2:22–23)

ST. PAUL'S DIRECTIONS FOR THE LIFE OF THE CHRISTIAN COMMUNITY (3:1—4:6)

I. Lift up your thoughts (3:1–4)

II. Put off the old self (3:5–9)

III. Clothed in the new self (3:10–11)

IV. A picture of the new self (3:12–16)
1. Tender compassion and kindness (3:12)
2. Readiness to forgive (3:13)
3. Charity and peace (3:14–15a)
4. Gratitude (3:15b)
5. The spiritual life of the new self (3:16)

V. Do everything in the Lord's name and giving thanks to God (3:17)

VI. A domestic program (3:18—4:1)
1. Wives (3:18)
2. Husbands (3:19)
3. Children (3:20)
4. Fathers (3:21)
5. Slaves (3:22–25)
6. Masters (4:1)

VII. Final exhortations (4:2–6)

1. Prayer and intercession (4:2–4)
2. Relations with others (4:5–6)

The Close of the Letter (4 : 7–18)

CONCLUSION (4:7–18)

I. Tychicus and Onesimus will give them news of Paul (4:7–9)

II. Greetings from the others (4:10–14)

III. Greetings to the brothers and sisters, and final instructions (4:15–17)

IV. Greetings in St. Paul's own handwriting (4:18a)

V. Good wishes (4:18b)

THE OPENING OF THE LETTER

(1:1-2)

INTRODUCTORY VERSES
(1:1–2)

The Sender (1:1)

[1a]*From Paul who is an apostle of Jesus Christ by God's will . . .*

Paul is not just any ordinary Christian; he is an apostle of Jesus Christ. He does not act or write on his own authority; he holds a commission from Jesus Christ, whom the Christians he is writing to acknowledge as their Lord. According to his own testimony, St. Paul received this commission before the gates of Damascus; Christ appeared to him in glory and appointed him as his "chosen instrument," to bring his name "before the heathen and their rulers, and before the people of Israel too" (Acts 9:15). It was then that he was "called to be Christ's apostle" (Rom. 1:1).

This was in accordance with God's purpose. As a Jew who was well versed in the scriptures, St. Paul had been convinced even before his "conversion" that he understood God's purpose sufficiently from the law, which he had studied so deeply. "In enthusiasm for the Jewish way of life, I surpassed many of my contemporaries among my own people. I was a fanatic for the traditions of my fathers" (Gal. 1:14). But now, before the city of Damascus, he experienced God's will in a completely new way; he experienced it now, not as a mere statement of God's demands, but as "a light from heaven" which threw him to the ground (Acts 9:3–4; 22:6; 26:13) and "set him apart to preach the gospel of God" (Rom. 1:1). This was the way the prophets and saints of the Old Testament had experienced God's will; they were solemnly pressed into its service. God's will may appear the same way to any ordinary Christian. It may seem "surprising" and appear as an unconditional summons to a particular task which may mean the end of the way of life a person was used to and to which he was attached. St. Paul writes as "an apostle of Jesus Christ," so that his words are those of one who is "sent." Consequently they are the words of the Lord himself. They are authoritative and have an obligatory character for the Christian community. We are bound to listen to them. Jesus Christ himself speaks through his apostle.

1b*. . . and the brother Timothy . . .*

Timothy appears with St. Paul as the second sender of the letter. He is his special "collaborator" (Rom. 16:21) and he is as close to him as "a son helping his father" (Philem. 2:22). We can see this also from the "and" which unites their names. He is the brother both of St. Paul and of the community. St. Paul names him as a co-sender of the letter, so that he shares in his apostolic authority. However, he is not "an apostle of Jesus Christ," nor is he set apart "by God's will." He stands between St. Paul and the different communities as a brother and in his devotion to both parties he serves to unite them. This gives us some idea of the essence of an office or ministry in the church.

The Addressees (1:2a)

2a*. . . to the saints at Colossae, the faithful brothers in Christ.*

The letter is addressed to the community at Colossae, a town on the upper Lycus in Phrygia. St. Paul himself had never worked there and the community was founded by Epaphras who was from Colossae (1:7; 4:12). It was he who informed St. Paul about the community and their spiritual state (1:8), with the result that he wrote them this letter.

In the address, St. Paul describes the Colossians as " saints " and " our faithful brothers in Christ." This description is very important; it enables us to understand how the Christians regarded themselves in those days and how they should regard themselves in our day. The title "saints" connects the Christian community with the " holy people " of the Old Testament to whom God addressed the command, " You must be holy, as I am holy " (Lev. 11:44). The people of Israel were " holy " and they were bound to be holy, because they had been set apart from other nations by God's mysterious choice of them. They belonged to him in a special way; they were his " possession." Now, however, it is the church of Jesus Christ which is God's holy people; they are " consecrated by the Holy Spirit " (Rom. 15:16) and sanctified through the blood of Christ (Heb. 13:12). In this way, the church became God's possession (Tit. 2:14). By addressing the Christians as " saints," St. Paul reminds them that God has chosen them, so that they are obliged to live a life which is in accordance with his will. As a result of God's choice of them, a community of Christians occupies an incomparable position among all the other social groups in the world.

The Colossians are also described as " our brethren who believe in Christ." They are brothers as well as " saints." That was what the Christians called themselves, just as the Jews had already done under the old law. This realization of the common brotherhood of the faithful reveals a vivid awareness of belonging together. It is based on their communion in Christ, " the eldest-born among many brethren " (Rom. 8:9); " he is not ashamed to call them [mankind] his brethren " (Heb. 2:11); he wanted to " become altogether like his brethren " (2:17). Christ is the foundation stone of a great new brotherhood among men and this brotherhood is already visible and active in the church. In time to come, the church will be above all a church of brotherhood, to an even greater extent than previously. As the congregation and assembly of " brethren," the church will always become more and more of a sign and a promise for humanity.

We can be sure that St. Paul's letter to the community at Colossae was read out when they came together for public worship (cf. 4:16), that is, to celebrate the Lord's Supper. That is the principal occasion on which the brotherhood which exists among Christ's faithful is demonstrated. It is there that this brotherhood is nourished with the flesh and blood of the Son of Man; it is there that it is experienced as a communion " in Christ." Christ is the center of this communion; it is from him and for him that it lives.

Greetings (1:2b)

2b*Grace and peace from God our Father be yours.*

The Greeks used to greet one another with the word " Joy " (*chara*), whereas the Jews used " Peace " (*shalom*). St. Paul greets his readers with both words, grace and peace. This is a Christianized form of greeting which wishes the readers God's gracious and benevolent favor, together with that peace which the world cannot give (Jn. 14:27). Grace and peace are inseparably connected with the salvation which God gives us in Christ. This peace had already been announced by the prophets of the Old

Testament for the coming age of salvation and it was proclaimed once again to the shepherds at Bethlehem (Lk. 2:14). Jesus Christ, the Messiah, " came, and proclaimed peace to you who were far away and peace to those who were near " (Eph. 2:17). This refers to the Jews and Gentiles; they have been reconciled and form a community of brothers in the church, the one body of Christ (Eph. 2:14–16).

According to Colossians 1:2, this proclamation of grace and peace which brings us salvation has its origin in the heavenly Father personally; it is he who caused " the good news of peace through Jesus Christ, the Lord of all, to be made known " (Acts 10:36). The message of peace brought by the New Testament includes the revelation of the goodness of God who is " our Father." Through Christ, who brings us this messianic peace, we all have " access " (Eph. 2:18) to him on equal terms, and all men experience their common brotherhood in him. This is demonstrated above all in the church's worship which is the assembly of all those who have become brothers, and should enable them to experience the truth of the words, " You are all brethren alike " (Mt. 23:28).

THE BODY OF THE LETTER
(1:3—4:6)

THE MYSTERY OF CHRIST
(1:3—2:23)

Nearly all of St. Paul's epistles have two parts, one of which is theological and doctrinal, while the other deals with practical behavior. The theological and doctrinal exposition always precedes the ethical considerations. It offers us a discussion of God's saving activity as it is revealed in history in Christ; this is the foundation of the Christian life; it gives us the facts of that life. The obligations of the Christian life, the imperative it imposes, with its moral demands and the need for truly Christian behavior, are a consequence of this. Christianity must never be confined to the level of "theory." The message we have received must be put into practice. This was one of Jesus' great concerns in his preaching.

From the text of sacred scripture a Christian must get an ever greater "insight" (1:9) into the mysteries of salvation, "to make us understand God's gift to us" (1 Cor. 2:12). It is of these that St. Paul speaks, "not, indeed, in words inspired by human wisdom, but in words such as the [Holy] Spirit teaches" (1 Cor. 2:13). By means of these words, he "makes every mind a prisoner in subjection to Christ" (2 Cor. 10:5). This insight gives rise to the joy and spirit of penance which is typical of a Christian; it inspires a change of heart and truly Christian behavior. This is what St. Paul wants to persuade the Colossians to do, and us with them. His letter is just as important for us as it was for that church in Asia Minor.

The "insight" which St. Paul wishes to communicate in the epistle to the Colossians refers especially to the "mystery of Christ," his position in the world of creation and of redemption. He is the center of all and St. Paul's thought revolves round him. It is his urgent wish that his readers' thoughts, too, should be centered on him; so they will be "firmly established" and "nothing will move them away from the hope they found in the gospel" (1:23).

St. Paul's Thanksgiving for the Community (1:3–8)

[3]*We give thanks at all times to God, the Father of our Lord Jesus Christ, in the prayer [we offer] for you.*

St. Paul's prayer is an expression of thanksgiving, and his thanksgiving is a prayer. This was in keeping with the Old Testament tradition of prayer with which he was familiar and which we find especially in the thanksgiving psalms:

> Give thanks to God, because he is good!
> His graciousness endures forever.
> So must those whom God has rescued say,
> those whom he rescued in their need,
> gathering them from the lands,
> from east and west, from north and south
> (Ps. 106:1–3).

St. Paul is not content with calling on the Colossians to give thanks to God (1:12; 3:17; 4:2); he gives thanks continually and his thanks are inspired by the thought of what God has done for the community. His unceasing thanks help us to realize that all his missionary efforts, as well as those of his helpers, were fruitful only because God had blessed them and made their work successful; "neither the one who plants nor the one who waters is important, but only God who gives the increase" (1 Cor. 3:7). That is why it is right to thank "the Father of our Lord Jesus Christ." It is God who gives us the gift of salvation through Jesus Christ and it is this salvation which is the content of the message Christian missionaries bring. What they hand on is a pure gift of God's grace and this is still true today and forever.

St. Paul's thanksgiving is also a prayer for them. His thanks are at the same time a form of intercession in which he remembers the community. In this way, St. Paul demonstrates his attachment to them. As a true pastor of souls, he bears the needs of the community before God the Father in his prayers and thanksgiving.

4 For we have heard of the faith you have while being in Christ Jesus and of the love which you cherish for all the saints . . .

St. Paul had reason for the thanks which he offers to God. Epaphras had brought him good news of the church at Colossae (1:9). For one thing, there was their lively faith in Jesus Christ. The Christian life is a life of faith. For St. Paul, faith is "nothing less than the knowledge of all that God has attached to the name and work of Christ." That is why he speaks here of the faith they have while being in Jesus Christ, and not of their belief in Christ himself. The faith which Christians share springs from their union with their Lord; it is in Christ's sphere that it lives. In this way, faith defines a very special manner of existence in the world and is its foundation; this is a mystery to the unbeliever; he cannot understand it and at times it can even be a stumbling block to him.

Such faith cannot and must not remain inactive. It must "find its expression in love" (Gal. 5:6). St. Paul sees that the Colossians' faith is like this; he has heard of the love which they cherish for all the saints. We can be sure Epaphras will have told him of the different proofs of their love which they had shown to the members of their own community and to others. It is possible that the Colossians had taken part in the great collection for the poor of the first Christian church at Jerusalem, which was so dear to St. Paul's heart. He sees in this an attitude of love which extends to all those who are brothers in the faith. True Christian love is all-embracing and knows no limits, like Jesus' love and the love of our heavenly Father. It is passionately interested in every case of need in the whole world. It is this which shows that Christians realize they are brothers and take it seriously; it is this which proves the sincerity of their life of faith. Christians in our own day are coming to understand this more and more; this makes the Christian faith credible to those who are "weak" in the faith and those who "are not of our company."

5a . . . *because of the hope which lies ready for you in heaven.*

The Colossians have good reason to insure that their faith should prove itself in love. The reason is the hope of what awaits them with God in heaven. Later St. Paul will tell us what this hope consists in. It is Christ himself who has been exalted and stands at God's right hand; our real "life" is now hidden with him (3:3f.). The hope which the Christian community enjoys is not a vague hope such as might be shared by the whole world; it is a solid, concrete hope, just as Christ himself is a concrete person and not a phantasm. It is the constant recollection of this hope which inspires the Colossians' faith, so that it brings forth fruit in works of love. Their hope is not regarded as a reward, but as the driving force behind their Christian attitude towards their brothers. When a Christian raises his thoughts to Christ "above" (3:1f.), this does not make him unfit for life in the world; on the contrary, it fits him for such a life; it gives him a social consciousness and makes him clear-sighted; so that he can see what must be done today and every day. Paradoxical as it may seem, this thought enables a person to behave as a true contemporary! It makes him conscious of his responsibility in time and for time.

In these verses of St. Paul, we can see the triple constellation which characterizes and determines the Christian life, faith, hope, and charity. It is within the co-ordinates formed by these three "theological" virtues that the Christian life develops. It is by means of them that a man gets out of himself. By faith he enters the sphere of the divine, the sphere of God's salvation in Christ; by hope he reaches out to grasp the perfection of that salvation which is to come; by love he renounces his own interests and devotes himself to others. By faith, hope, and charity, a person is enabled to give new dimensions to his activity for time and eternity.

5b *You have already heard about this hope in the true message of the gospel . . .*

The gospel proclaims that a person must have hope. It tells us that God has opened himself to men in Christ in order to save them. "Brothers, we have an assured hope of entering into the [heavenly] sanctuary, in virtue of Jesus' blood" (Heb. 10:19). Jesus' death "for us" gives the world hope. The Colossians have been told of this already, when the gospel was preached to them. "We have a mind to flee for refuge and take a firm grasp on the hope offered us, in which we have a safe and firm anchor for our souls reaching in to what is behind the veil" (Heb. 6:18b–19). It is of this that the gospel speaks and its message is truth-giving. The gospel contains God's promise and his word is true and worthy of trust; he has the power to fulfill his promises. In the whole world, there is nothing so true as the message of the gospel.

6. *. . which came to you; it bears abundant fruit and increases in you, as it does in the whole world, from the day on which you heard of God's grace and truly recognized it . . .*

The gospel "came to" the Colossians, too, one day. They received its truth-giving message and the hope it brings. That was a red-letter day for the people of Colossae and now the gospel has become an indispensable factor in their midst and it produces its effects. St. Paul speaks of the gospel as a mysterious entity and power, and it is only later that he tells us who brought it to Colossae. The gospel is certainly greater and more powerful than the missionary who brings it; Christ himself is present in it, offering himself to men as the One who brings salvation. The gospel takes his place; it "represents" our Lord and tells us about the salvation he brings.

The gospel has reached Colossae and bears fruit there as it does in the whole world. St. Paul was perfectly entitled to make this claim, when he wrote this epistle. "The whole world" was for him the Roman Empire and it was he himself who had made the gospel known in the most important parts of it, especially in Asia Minor and Greece. With joyful gratitude, he could claim that it was bearing fruit and taking root everywhere. The gospel is like the grain of mustard seed in Jesus' parable (Mk. 4:30–32). Its beginnings were insignificant, but now the tree is already bearing abundant fruit. Moreover, it is still growing and will bear still more fruit in the future. St. Paul abstracts completely from his own missionary labors, and so he makes no mention of the failures, setbacks, and persecutions which he had to endure in the service of the gospel. He allows himself to be completely overshadowed by the object which he serves as an apostle. The numerous churches which he and others had established "the world over" are irrefutable proof of the divine power of the gospel. Every Christian community is a fruit of the gospel and a living proof of its power.

This was true also of Colossae; there too the gospel had brought forth rich fruit "from the day on which you heard of God's grace and truly recognized it." God's grace is the essential content of the gospel, its essence; this is revealed in Christ, in his redeeming death, and in his being raised from the dead. The gospel announces this to the whole world. The wonderful thing is that God's grace can be heard in the gospel and recognized for what it is, as happened at Colossae. Since then, the phrase "the world over" has gained a wider meaning and this miracle is still being performed. For this, all we can do is to thank God continually in the church.

Hearing of does not necessarily mean recognizing. The Colossians did both. Hearing means listening to the preaching of the gospel with concentration and attention; recognizing it means penetrating into its message with understanding and giving it assent. This gives rise to the insight: Certainly, God was truly at work in Jesus' death on the cross. Faith means assenting to what God does and accepting what we are told about him.

7*. . . as you have learned [it] from Epaphras our beloved fellow slave. He is a loyal minister of Christ in our stead.*

St. Paul is so intent on God's gift, the gospel, that he feels compelled to speak of it first, before saying who brought it to the Colossians. This was Epaphras, who was from Colossae. He is a well-loved fellow bondsman of St. Paul, and he shared his imprisonment (Philem. 23). He had worked as a missionary in Colossae, Laodicea, and Hierapolis (4:12f.), perhaps at the direction of St. Paul. This would mean that St. Paul could consider the towns in that area as belonging to his mission territory. This would obviously give him the right to send letters to the Christians at Colossae and Laodicea (4:17).

Epaphras was the teacher from whom they learned the gospel. Just as the apostles had once been to "school" with Jesus, so now the Colossians must go to school to the gospel, through Epaphras. In this school a person learns how to recognize God's ways of salvation and God himself in them; he learns how to be a disciple of Jesus and become "perfect in Christ" (1:28). There is such a thing as "learning Christ" (Eph. 4:20) and this school lasts a lifetime.

Epaphras proved himself a loyal minister (deacon) of Jesus Christ in Paul's place. A missionary is in the immediate service of Christ, as his loyal minister; he proclaims Christ's saving activity in the world and makes it present among men. However, he cannot take it upon himself to preach; he can do so only in dependence on the church founded on the apostles. The church sends him out as a missionary in Christ's name. In his mission territory, Epaphras represented St. Paul; he worked "in our place" ("for us"). In other words, he worked in conscious and voluntary communion with St. Paul and in dependence upon him. In this way, the union of doctrine and love between the communities evangelized and the founders of the church is preserved. The church continues to be "apostolic" and this is essential to it.

8 *It was he who told us of your love in the Spirit.*

Epaphras was with St. Paul at this time (4:12f.) and he gave him news about the spiritual state of his communities. This too was necessary for the preservation of unity in the church, which could not be allowed to be lost. That was how St. Paul heard of the " love in the Spirit " which the Colossians cherished. This does not refer to their attachment to him personally; it refers to the new basic disposition, the new communion and community consciousness which the Holy Spirit himself promotes in the church. In the church, each one exists for the others, and each community for the other communities, and all exist for Christ. St. Ignatius, the bishop of Antioch, later referred to the church at Rome as the church which presides in love; with these words he touched on the deepest essence of the church.

St. Paul, therefore, had reason to remember the church at Colossae with gratitude in his prayer to God. All that he has said about it in the detailed description which he gives in his letter so far gives us an authentic picture of a Christian community. If it can be said of a community that it is characterized by faith, hope, and charity, it deserves to be called " Christian." But even a genuinely Christian community such as this cannot afford to mark time; they must still " bear fruit in every good work, growing through closer knowledge of God " (1 : 10). That this may be achieved among the Colossians is the purpose of the doctrinal exposition which St. Paul gives us in the following verses.

The Object of His Prayer; Deeper Insight into the Salvation Which Is Accorded Them, and Joyful Gratitude for It (1:9–13)

9a *Therefore, we have never ceased, from the day we heard the news, to pray and offer entreaty for you . . .*

If the community is to get on well in the school of the gospel, it needs prayer and intercession, especially the intercession of those who are its pastors and superiors. St. Paul realizes this, and so he repeatedly assures his readers of his incessant prayer on their behalf as their apostle. In this way, even a community with which he was not personally acquainted, such as that at Colossae, remained in close union with him. The result was a communion of prayer which was never to be destroyed. St. Paul wants to pray " unceasingly " for the community. The repetition, " praying," " offering entreaty," shows us how fervent his intercession was.

9b*. . . that you may be filled with the knowledge of his will, in all wisdom and spiritual insight . . .*

St. Paul was a Jew and had been a zealous Pharisee. For a Jew, knowledge and action are one in religious matters. What is known (from the law) must be put into practice. That was why pious Jews were so eager to know God's will. St. Paul was still influenced by this problem even as a Christian and he makes this desire a theme of his prayer for his communities. He prays that they may be filled with the knowledge of God's will, so that " theory " and " practice " will be identical in their case too. This is a sure sign of a genuine and trustworthy Christian. Christian faith, without " growth in all good " (1 : 10), would be absurd and impious for St. Paul.

This knowledge of God's will is had in all wisdom and all spiritual insight. There is no doubt that the knowledge of God's will can at times be obscured, as was the case with the Pharisees. Our Lord had to struggle bitterly against such deviations. The knowledge of God's will which a Christian should have is not the result of hair-splitting and casuistry in explaining the " letter " of the law; it comes instead from listening attentively to God's word and the voice of his Spirit in our hearts. This insight, which is due to the influence of the Spirit, enables a person to act according to God's will in all wisdom. It presupposes a lively sense of what objective reality demands. Such insight can be obtained only by persevering prayer.

10a. . . *so that you may walk worthy of the Lord, in a way which will find approval, . . .*

God's will must be known and put into practice, literally, in a person's walking, that is, in his whole life. St. Paul often uses the expression "walking " (" walking about," " wandering "). The idea at the back of his mind is the biblical notion that man is on the way, that his life is like a journey which leads to salvation or damnation.

St. Paul's prayer is that a Christian's whole life must be worthy of the Lord. The Lord is Jesus Christ. When is a Christian's life such as befits his servant? The best answer to this question is to be found in those other passages of St. Paul's epistles where he describes this " walking " in greater detail; they should " walk," " in the spirit " (Gal. 5:16), " as men native to the light " (Eph. 5:8), " in good actions " (Eph. 2:10), " in a new kind of existence " (Rom. 6:4), " prudently " (Col. 4:5), " in charity " (Eph. 5:2). In this way a Christian's life is worthy of the Lord who died for us " and left us his own example; we were to walk in his footsteps " (1 Pet. 2:21). A disciple who really imitates Jesus walks worthy of his master.

A Christian, moreover, spends his life in a way which will find approval. He does not travel alone; he is accompanied by his brothers in the community of the church, including those who are " weak." Their lives are lived in full view of God and the world. If a Christian is worthy of his Lord, it gives pleasure to God and men. His life has a missionary effect; it makes Christianity appear worthy of faith. " Let your light shine before men so that they can see your good works, and glorify your Father who is in heaven " (Mt. 5:16). " Behave prudently towards those who are not of your company " (Col. 4:5). Those who are " weak " in the community will be strengthened by the good example of those who are " strong."

10b. . . *bearing fruit in every good work and growing in the knowledge of God, . . .*

St. Paul explains more clearly what he means by a life which is " worthy of the Lord." It bears fruit in every good work, as it is bound to do. He leaves it to the imagination of his Christian readers to decide what good works they should do in practice, so that their lives may be fruitful. In the second part of his letter, he gives as many examples as are needed. The idea of " fruitfulness " is connected with the image of a " tree " which our Lord used in the sermon on the mount. A tree can be good or bad and it bears fruit accordingly (Mt. 7:17–20). The thought of good fruit will remind a Christian reader especially of the " fruit of the Spirit " which St. Paul describes in the epistle to the Galatians: love, joy, peace, patience, kindness, generosity, faith, gentleness, temperateness (Gal. 5:22).

St. Paul speaks also of growth in the knowledge of God. In himself, God is " a God of hidden ways " (Is. 45:15), but he revealed " his eternal power and his divineness " in creation, so that men might have knowledge of him (Rom. 1:20). His justice, which justifies the sinner, was "revealed" (Rom. 1:17) to the eyes of faith in the gospel. His glory shines in the features of Jesus Christ (2 Cor. 4:6; Jn. 14:9). God's incarnate Son has told us about him (Jn. 1:18). However, God's being remains an unfathomable mystery even for a Christian; eternity itself will not be sufficient to enable us to exhaust it. "Closer knowledge of God," therefore, involves two things, the knowledge that God is an impenetrable mystery, and the knowledge of all that he has revealed to us about this mystery through his Spirit. Only the Spirit knows "what is in God," "the depths of God's nature" (1 Cor. 2:10–12). Such knowledge of God brings a person into contact with his mystery and gives him cause for happiness. And St. Paul prays that his Christians may grow in it. There is nothing which can make a person happier or more blessed than the knowledge of God. . . . Consequently many spiritual masters teach that contemplation takes precedence over action.

11 *. . . strengthened with all power according to the might of his glory, in all patience and endurance.*

St. Paul's thoughts are overloaded; his words and sentences jostle one another, they are so full of meaning. However, they are all worth meditating on.

When a person realizes that knowledge of God is the whole point of man's life on earth, he may become impatient. Life in the body and in the world seems to separate him from the "object" of his knowledge; "My desire is to depart and be with Christ" (Phil. 1:23). Therefore, a Christian needs to practice patience and endurance; these will enable him to persevere in this world of death. In order to accomplish this, he will need special strength from God.

[12a]*That you [moreover] may give joyful thanks to the Father . . .*

St. Paul himself offers thanks (1:3) to the heavenly Father unceasingly, and it is the object of his prayer that the Colossians and all Christians should do likewise. Where could this be done more fittingly than in the great Thanksgiving, the celebration of the Eucharist? This thanksgiving must be joyful, as we read of the members of the first community at Jerusalem, " They broke bread ... and took their meal with gladness and simplicity of heart" (Acts 2:46). Such gratitude is the result of knowledge; it is a result of the knowledge of God's saving activity in Christ, which is proclaimed and celebrated in the liturgical assembly. Those who are redeemed have received knowledge and this gives them cause to thank the heavenly Father joyfully. His goodness has been revealed in the work of our redemption. The thanks offered by a person who has been redeemed is the thanks of a child to his Father. "The more strongly flows the stream of grace, the more hearts should overflow with gratitude, to God's honor" (2 Cor. 4:15).

[12b]*. . . who has made you capable of sharing the inheritance of the saints in the light;* [13]*and freed us from the power of darkness and transferred us to the kingdom of the Son he loves.*

In three short phrases, St. Paul tells us how God has manifested his fatherly goodness to us in the redemption. He has made us capable of sharing the inheritance of the saints in the light. The "light" means God's kingdom, which we usually call "heaven." There an inheritance awaits the saints, that is, the faithful—the hope mentioned in verse 5, the hope prepared for them by God himself. The curse of death which held sway over all that exists on earth has been removed by God. In baptism

God makes the faithful "fit" to pass over from death to life (Jn. 5:24), from the kingdom of darkness and death to the kingdom of God's light and glory. St. Paul himself continues, "He freed us from the power of darkness." In these words, he has baptism in mind; he sees in it an act by which God rescues us. The "power of darkness" is the devil's sphere of influence, where death lies in wait on the horizon. In his third phrase, St. Paul returns to a positive idea, "He has transferred us to the kingdom of the Son he loves." This, too, has reference to baptism.

The burden of St. Paul's preaching was that God raised Jesus Christ from the dead and made him sit at his right hand in heaven, and this was the usual approach in the early church. In baptism God has raised us up too and enthroned us too in heaven, in and with Christ (Eph. 2:6), so that "the saints [the heavenly beings] are our fellow citizens and we belong to God's household" (Eph. 2:19). These are not just pious or poetical expressions St. Paul uses; they are statements which are meant in all seriousness; they reveal the mystery of our Christian existence. He calls this kingdom where Christ rules, where his influence and love reign supreme, "the kingdom of his [God's] beloved Son," and it is to this that God has transferred us in baptism. In other passages of his epistles, St. Paul describes this mystery briefly as existence in Christ. It is a mystery of faith and practice . . . It is the motive of a Christian's joy and gratitude . . . It is the spiritual experience which should result from the proper celebration of the liturgy . . . The mystery of the church . . .

Later it will become clear why St. Paul speaks of this "Christ-mystery" of our existence in faith and in the church, in the Epistle to the Colossians. He had good reason to do so.

The mention of the Son gives St. Paul his decisive cue; it prompts him to describe Christ's place in the world of creation and of redemption without waiting any longer. He does this in a form of hymn which serves at the same time as a basis from which he can launch an attack on the opinions of the "Colossian heretics." His teaching, however, is valid for all time.

A "Christological Hymn" (1:14–20)

Redemption through Christ (1:14)

14 *It is in him we enjoy redemption, the forgiveness of sins.*

The phrase "in him" which St. Paul uses in this verse refers to God's beloved Son (v. 13). The conviction of our faith that we enjoy redemption is founded in him alone; he died for us. The Jews looked for a day of redemption to come in the future but, as a Christian, St. Paul knows that we have already "found" redemption and the church shares this conviction, because the Redeemer has already come in the person of Jesus Christ. This "enjoying" ("having") is an expression of the certainty of our faith, a certainty which gives us cause for happiness.

The most important element in redemption is mentioned immediately, the forgiveness of sins, their remission. God forgives us our sins; that means he does not look at them any more, he covers them up. Indeed, he obliterates them, because someone else has died for us sinners. The Redeemer is the Crucified; on the cross he cancelled the deed on which our sins appeared (Col. 2:14). When redemption and forgiveness of sin are mentioned, a Christian naturally thinks of Jesus' cross.

Christ the True Likeness of the Invisible God, the Firstborn of All Creation (1:15)

15 *He is the image of the invisible God, the firstborn before all creation.*

God dwells in "unapproachable light; no human being has seen or can ever see him" (1 Tim. 6:16). For those who have faith, however, God has let his light shine in Christ's features (2 Cor. 4:6); as his incarnate Son, he is God's image. The features of the invisible God have become visible in the features of Christ, so that when we look at him we see the Father (Jn. 14:9). Jesus Christ reveals the Father to us; in him God leaves aside his reserve. But St. Paul wants to tell us more. In the Old Testament divine wisdom is described as "the glow that radiates from eternal light," "the mirror of God's majesty," "the faithful image of his goodness" (Wisd. 7:26). Wisdom was present when God made heaven and earth (Prov. 8:22–31) and it pitched its tent in Israel (Sir. 24:8). At a very early period, Christians had already applied the Old Testament references to divine wisdom to Jesus Christ. He is the eternal Word of God, through whom all things were made and he pitched his tent among us (Jn. 1:1–14). Christ as the image of the invisible God should remind us also of the wonder and glory of creation, as well as of the miracle of the Incarnation of the eternal Word in Christ. God's wisdom has become visible in Jesus Christ in person; he is God's "image." An image fashioned by a great master can mean a lot to a man; it can portray the whole world for him, an ideal world. Similarly, a Christian sees God's world portrayed in Christ who is the image of the God we cannot see.

The Old Testament regards wisdom as God's firstborn (Prov.

8:22–31); wisdom was already there when God created the world. Under the guidance of the Holy Spirit, the church realized that Jesus Christ, God's incarnate Son and his image, is this wisdom. That is why St. Paul and the church refer to him as the firstborn before all creation; it is not as if Christ were the first creature created by God; this title merely serves to proclaim the dignity which he enjoys as the Ruler of all creation.

What St. Paul tells us about Christ in this hymn (1:15–20) reveals his essence to us. Such a text is meant to be prayed aloud and sung (cf. 3:16). In this way, these expressions which testify to our faith become a prayer of adoration and praise to the Lord. Reflection on the sacred text should lead to the same result.

Creation in Christ (1:16)

16*For everything was created in him, in heaven and on earth, visible and invisible, thrones and dominations, authorities and powers. Everything was created through him and for him.*

The exalted dignity of the position Christ occupies in creation as a whole and the superiority he enjoys as its Ruler are based on the fact that everything was created through him and in him and for him. This is what St. Paul wishes to emphasize; it is to this that he wishes to draw our attention, that is, to Christ. He is the beginning, the center and the goal of all creation.

The pagan religions used to speak in similar terms. In contrast to them and in full agreement with the Old Testament and the faith of the church, St. Paul does not tell us that everything merely "exists" in him; he says everything was created in him. This emphasizes the clear and unequivocal distinction between the Creator and what he creates. This universe is his free creation and it had a beginning in time. At the same time, it is still in his hands, it is encompassed by his power, because it was created by God in Christ. What being "created in him" means for the universe is something which we can scarcely fathom in this life. The "Christ-mystery" which is involved in creation transcends our earthly power of understanding and can be conceived only in faith. However, we can see at least that this means creation is good, that it is a whole, that it is not meaningless. This is the source of the light which illuminates the essence of the universe and of its intelligibility for the human spirit. In creation the human spirit can and should learn to recognize the Creator, his eternal power and his divineness (Rom. 1:20). Creation should lead man to adore the Creator.

There was a tendency among the Colossians not to take Christ's rule over creation at its full value. The temptation has always been great—and still is—to exclude certain areas of creation from his dominion and see something " diabolical " in them (cf. 2:8, 16–23). That is why St. Paul places such emphasis on the fact that everything was created in Christ, everything without exception " in heaven and on earth, visible and invisible." Among these are included especially the heavenly beings, the angels, of which he names a number of "classes." If he had been writing today, St. Paul would perhaps have mentioned other different elements and areas of creation which might seem " diabolical " to men, and yet they too were all created " in Christ "; such areas are, for example, the depths of space or the depths of the human soul, as modern science reveals them to us. The " powers " of history are also subject to Christ. Faith in Christ who has been raised to glory gives us confidence in creation; it enables us to deal with its forces without misgiving.

Only Satan and his accomplices are enemies of creation (Apoc. 12:12); it is they who " corrupt the world " (Apoc. 11:18).

" Everything was created through him and for him." This principle is valid for all time and, moreover, it reveals another mystery of creation. Because God created the universe *through* the Word (Jn. 1:3), it owes its origin and its continued existence to Christ. Because it was created *for* him, the universe does not run its course in a night of absurdity and unreality; it has a goal, the eternal Christ and his glory. God has instilled in it the hope that it too " will be set free from the slavery of corruption, to share in the glorious freedom of God's sons," even though it still " groans in travail " and is surrounded by death and nothingness (Rom. 8:20-22). Christ is the salvation of the whole universe. The church gives expression to this faith and hope by adapting many of the things of nature to sacred purposes in the liturgy, such as light, wax, fire, incense, water, salt, oil, ash, air and breath, saliva, earth, bread and wine, as well as man himself. In the liturgy the restoration of creation has already begun.

Christ Takes Precedence over All (1:17)

17 *And HE is before everything, and everything subsists in him.*

The reference to Christ sounds almost like a solemn formula of revelation. It is emphasized by being put at the beginning of the sentence in this verse of the hymn, " It is HE who is before everything." This must be taken as referring primarily to the chronological order, but it also refers to the rank Christ enjoys. He precedes everything else in the order of time and so he is also infinitely superior to everything else, and not just initially but forever; he takes precedence. . . . It is more important to remember this today than ever before. The world with all its magnificence occupies an ever larger place in modern man's consciousness. Progress in our understanding of the incredible vastness of the universe and its conquest by science are among the causes of this. But Christ always takes precedence over it; he is superior to the universe.

Everything subsists in him. It is Christ who gives cohesion to everything in its innermost being. Christ is the ultimate reason for the existence of all creation. This is a mystery we cannot hope to penetrate in this life. " We are determined to praise him still; for we cannot fathom him; he is greater than all his works " (Sir. 43:28).

The Head of This Body, the Firstborn of the Dead (1:18)

18 *And HE is the head of the body, the church, for he is the beginning, the firstborn from the dead, so that HE may be the first in every way.*

In the preceding verses of the hymn, St. Paul drew our attention to the mystery of Christ and creation; now he draws it to the mystery of the church. As he himself explains, the church is the body of which Christ is the Head. The image of the church as the body of Christ gives us a deep insight into its mystery. It enables us to see the indissoluble communion of " destiny " which exists between the church and Christ its Head, a deep interior communion. As " Head," Christ is Lord over the church and the church is subject to him in love (Eph. 5:23–24). He is the source of all its supernatural growth. It is " by him that the whole body is organized and held together " (Eph. 4:16). He " keeps it fed and warmed " (Eph. 5:29), especially by the sacraments of baptism and the Eucharist. When the faithful share the eucharistic meal in common, the mystery of the church as Christ's body is given visible form. " Because the bread is one, we, the many, form one body; we all share the same bread " (1 Cor. 10:17). The essence of the church is more clearly revealed at the Lord's table, in the celebration of the liturgy, than on any other occasion.

Jesus Christ, the Head of the church, was raised from the dead by God, and the members of his body, the faithful, will also be raised from the dead one day. Indeed, they have already been " raised with " Christ (2:12; Eph. 2:6) in baptism. In baptism they have already received a share in the divine life of Christ who rose from the dead (Eph. 2:5). That is why St. Paul can testify that Christ is the beginning, the firstborn of the dead. With him a fresh humanity begins, a humanity which is congregated in his " body." He is the second Adam, the living Adam who was promised for the last stage of time (cf. 1 Cor. 15:45-48). As the firstborn of the dead, Christ is the founder of a new line of succession, the new generation made up of those who were raised up with him. He is " the eldest-born among many brethren " (Rom. 8:29) and these have already been rescued in principle from the power of death. In Christ's body, God's " sphere of life " already penetrates into this world; " heaven " is already among us (cf. 1:13; Eph. 2:6).

In Hebrew the word for " head " (*rosch*) also meant " beginning." When Christ is described as the beginning (of the new creation), this serves also to emphasize the fact that, as such, he is the Head and Ruler of his brothers. St. Paul now says this explicitly; he is the " beginning, the firstborn of the dead; so that he may be first in every way "; he takes first place. We can be sure St. Paul is thinking here of Christ's exaltation to God's throne in heaven. Such an honor was his right, because everything was created in him. Christ is the Lord and life-giving principle of the new creation, just as he was in the first creation. But he enjoys this position in the new creation as a human being who has been raised to glory and is our brother. The Colossians were not sufficiently conscious of this, as many Christians are not sufficiently conscious of it today.

Christ Possesses God's "Fullness" (1:19)

[19]*For it was [God's] plan to let all fullness dwell in him . . .*

Christ's primacy of all and over all is the result of God's choice. It was God's good pleasure to let all his divine fullness dwell in him (cf. 2:9). It is probable that the Colossians had looked elsewhere for the " fullness " of God's power to bless and save; they may have sought it in the " elements of the world " (2:8, 20), in the mysteriously interwoven realities of nature and their powers, as many do today. That is why St. Paul tells them that God's infinite completeness dwells in the incarnate Lord who has been exalted in glory. Consequently, true and lasting salvation can come only from him.

All-Encompassing Reconciliation through Him (1:20)

[20]*. . . and, through him, to reconcile everything with himself, after he had made peace by the blood of his cross—[to reconcile everything] through him, whether on earth or in heaven.*

When we hear of "reconciliation" ("winning back"), we immediately think of sin. That is not the way with St. Paul. Reconciliation is necessary where formerly there had been hostility, so that peace results. Men are inclined to regard God as their enemy, because they live "a life of sin." God, on the other hand, has no thought of acting as man's enemy. On the contrary, St. Paul tells his readers, "We entreat you in Christ's name, be reconciled with God" (2 Cor. 5:20). In other words, give up the pagan idea that God is your enemy. Jesus' death on the cross is more than sufficient proof that God is man's friend and that he wants to be man's friend. "Even for a just man, scarcely anyone will lay down his life, although it is possible that someone may die on behalf of a good man. God, on the other hand, has proved his love to us by the fact that Christ died for us while we were still sinners . . . If we were reconciled with God by the death of his Son, while we were still sinners, how much more shall we not be saved in his life, now that we have been reconciled with him" (Rom. 5:7, 8, 10). God was not man's enemy, but man was God's enemy.

God wants to win back "all things through Christ" (1:20). The words "all things" show us that St. Paul is not thinking only of God's relations with man. There are other forms of hostility of the most varied and far-reaching kinds. It can be found among the different religions and peoples and especially in the world of the spirit and the world of spirits. Knowledge of history teaches us this continually.

God's work of reconciliation is accomplished through Christ and it is aimed at winning back everything into union with him. The world was created "for him" (1:16b) and so too the elimination of all hostility is aimed at union with him, who is our peace in his own person (Eph. 2:14a). He made "peace through his blood, shed on the cross, for everyone," no matter who they may be, no matter what race or religion they may belong to. He has " torn down the partition which separated us, and annulled our enmity . . . He came and proclaimed peace for you who were far off and peace for those who were near " (Eph. 2:14, 17). Christ is the world's great peacemaker; his cross is the source of peace and an invitation to it. His blood is its guarantee. This too is proclaimed to us every time the Eucharist is celebrated. There everyone, no matter what his state or his nationality, has the same " access to the Father " (Eph. 2:18).

St. Paul adds the mysterious remark that Christ's work of reconciliation is effective even in heaven. He may be thinking of the " princedoms and powers," " the spiritual powers of evil in the heavens " (Eph. 6:12) which he mentions elsewhere, or of Satan's power which has already received its death-blow through Christ's death on the cross. In any case, this passage represents a tremendous vision of the peace which Christ brings, which envelops the farthest reaches of space and time. In our lives, this must find an echo in our determined will to promote peace.

The Colossians Are Reconciled through Christ (1:21–23)

[21]*You, too, who were once estranged and hostilely disposed, as a result of your evil actions,* [22]*he has now reconciled in the body of his flesh by his death, to present you holy and undefiled and blameless before him.*

St. Paul now wants to make it clear to the Colossians that they too are included in Christ's work of reconciliation; they too . . . have been reconciled. " Once," that is, before their baptism, not only did they live in fear and terror of the demons and an inscrutable " fate "; they were really " estranged " from the true God. To their pagan mentality God was an enemy and their attitude towards him was one of hostility. Their consciences were uneasy because of their evil deeds, and so they thought they should try to placate the Supreme Being by all kinds of pagan practices of a magical and superstitious nature. " Now," however, things are different. Now they have listened to the gospel which tells them of their redemption by Christ (1:6). Now they have been reconciled with God through Christ, who died for them. There is no doubt that the message of the gospel may seem incredible to pagan ears; the Colossians failed to grasp its meaning fully, as various erroneous opinions within the community show (2:8, 16–23). That is why St. Paul tells them explicitly that the message of reconciliation concerns them too, as it also concerns us. It takes courage to really believe in the unbelievable message of the gospel.

Christ's reconciliation is not merely a message which brings good news; it also has a moral goal. This is man's sanctification, which is a continual task, so that Christ can eventually present him before the throne of the divine Judge as one who has been sanctified through his action. The gospel always implies an invitation to put it into practice, to confirm one's assent to it by one's moral life. It is a law, but a " spiritual law " (Rom. 8:2).

23 *Only you must persevere in the faith, well-grounded and steadfast; you must not be moved away from the hope the gospel you listened to brings, that gospel which has been preached through-*

out the whole of creation under heaven, of which I, Paul, have become the minister.

St. Paul has already praised the Colossians' faith (1:4). Yet he is moved to encourage them to persevere in the faith. The context shows that he is thinking especially of faith in their reconciliation through Christ. Faith can lose its lustre and become weak, as daily experience shows both in ourselves and in Christian communities. A Christian community is certainly "well-grounded" and "firmly established"; "it is built up on the foundation of the apostles and prophets in which Christ Jesus himself is the cornerstone" (Eph. 2:20). Nevertheless, it is the constant duty of such a community to become ever more "well-grounded and firmly established" in the faith and through the faith; "we are no longer to be immature, storm-tossed and driven here and there by every wind of doctrine invented by human deceit and cunning which is in the service of error" (Eph. 4:14). A Christian must pray unceasingly to God for steadfastness in the faith.

Only a person who is "firmly established" in the faith will be able to stand firm in the face of the difficulties and assaults he will meet from within and without, so that nothing will move him away from the hope the gospel brings. The gospel to which the Colossians and we ourselves listened brought a message of hope (1:5); the gospel itself is thus the hope of the world and of all creation (Rom. 8:19ff.). In St. Paul's surprisingly audacious phrase, it has been "preached to all creation under heaven." He was entitled to say this; from his prison he could look back over a life of extensive missionary activity which had brought him or his co-workers to almost every part of the then known world (cf. 1:6). Moreover, he was convinced that with the proclamation of the gospel an irresistible force has been introduced into the world which no power on earth can contain or bring to a halt. There is no imprisoning the word of God (2 Tim. 2:9b); it must " run its course triumphantly " (2 Thess. 3:1). Paul is a " deacon " of the word; even though he was called to be an apostle of Jesus Christ, he is a " servant " of the gospel and not its master. On the contrary, the gospel is his master; Christ has brought him into its service. The church too is a servant of the gospel, not its master.

St. Paul Proclaims and Executes God's "Secret" (1:24–28)

St. Paul's Happiness in His Suffering for the Church

24 *At the moment, I am happy in my sufferings for you, and I fill up in my own flesh what still remains to be filled of Christ's sufferings, for the benefit of his body which is the church.*

The work of an apostle and missionary in the service of the gospel is full of suffering. St. Paul knew this from his own experience and he speaks of it repeatedly in his letters. He gives a particularly detailed description of his " countless apostolic labors " in 2 Corinthians 11:23b–33. " I believe that God has obviously put us apostles in the last place, like men marked out for death " (1 Cor. 4:9a). " I bear the scars of the Lord Jesus stamped on my body " (Gal. 6:17b). The scars on his body are a visible proof of his suffering as an apostle. Yet he is glad of his sufferings, because they are " on your behalf." They bring a blessing on his communities and readers. " I am full of consolation, overflowing with happiness in all our distress" (1 Cor. 7:4b). "Yes, even if I must shed my blood as an offering to consecrate your faith, I am still glad and I share my happiness with you all" (Phil. 2:17).

In his own sufferings, St. Paul felt that "the sufferings of Christ overflowed into his life" (2 Cor. 1:5a). Therefore, he regarded them as a grace and a share in Christ's suffering. That was why he could write to the Colossians that, by suffering in his own person, he helped to "pay off" the debt which the afflictions of Christ still "leave to be paid," for the sake of the church. Christ continues to suffer in the members of his "body," the church, and St. Paul is not afraid to deputize for the church and take its place in his sufferings; he does it gladly.

Here we see a profound and mysterious communion of suffering which exists between Christ and his representative, St. Paul, and the church. There can be no doubt that this is a plentiful source of graces and blessings for the church and the whole of humanity. The sufferings and afflictions which Christians have to bear are not merely their own "private" concern; they have a "social" character; they benefit everybody. Suffering is never in vain, so that St. Paul can say to the Philippians, "You, too, should be glad and share your happiness with me" (Phil. 2:18).

St. Paul's Preaching as the Revelation of a "Secret" (1:25–26)

25 *I became a servant of the church as a result of the office God gave me for your benefit, to complete God's word, . . .*

"I am only executing a commission" (1 Cor. 9:17). This is how

St. Paul looks at his duty as an apostle; he regards it as a " stewardship " entrusted to him by God. This is what the Greek term which he uses (*oikonomia*) means. The office with which he has been entrusted makes him a servant of the church, not a ruler in it. In his view, his office places him at the service of two different masters; he is in the service of God and of the church. His office, therefore, is nothing more than a form of service, and he himself is nothing more than a " deacon " (minister) (cf. 1 Cor. 3:5). This is the way all offices in the church should be regarded; they are always " for your benefit."

St. Paul's " office of service " pursues an exalted goal, " to complete God's word among you." It is extraordinary that St. Paul should speak of completing God's word, with reference to his own office. However, the phrase helps us to realize that for him the gospel—that is what God's word means here—is primarily a promise which is addressed to the Colossians and to all those who listen to it. Together with the church, he himself " completes " this promise by fulfilling the duties of his office of service. " Completing " a promise means seeing that it becomes a reality. The gospel is not complete with the mere preaching of the word; the word leads to salvation here and now and everywhere the gospel is preached.

26. . . *the secret which was hidden from all ages and generations, but has now been revealed to his saints.*

God's word contains a secret which was hidden " in God " until now (Eph. 3:9b). " Now " he has revealed it for the first time " in the church " (Eph. 3:10), although, humanly speaking, he " knew " about it always. The secret in question is the secret which brings salvation to the gentiles (1:27), and these words of St. Paul show that "salvation" is not just an "afterthought," an "appendage" which God tacks on to creation; God laid his plans for salvation "before the foundation of the world" (Eph. 1:4–5). Salvation was the goal of the universe from the very beginning; it was created only to be saved.

The "saints"—that is, Christians who share the faith (1:2)—already know this secret which is contained in the gospel; St. Paul told them about it in the course of his apostolic activity. In accordance with God's will, "now" is the time when it is to be revealed. Consequently, the present period of time is also the last period, because the precise content of the "secret" is Christ, whom St. Paul preaches to the gentiles. By listening to the gospel, a Christian learns the ultimate secret of history.

The Secret: "Christ in You" (1:27)

27 *God determined to make known to them in what the wealth of the glory of this secret among the gentiles consists: Christ among [in] you, the hope of glory.*

The "secret" of God's plan of salvation which is revealed in the last stage of time concerns the "nations." That is what the gentiles are called in the Old Testament, in contrast to the Israelites. In concise but unusually pregnant terms, St. Paul now tells us what this secret is; it is Christ among (in) them. The Greek text of the epistle is intentionally undecided. It may mean Christ "among" them or Christ "in" them. We can be sure St. Paul meant both; Christ is "among" them as the Lord of the nations who was promised for the last period of time, and Christ is " in " them because of his intimate union with the community through faith and baptism.

As a result of Christian missionary activity, the nations of the earth are drawn into Christ's " sphere of influence," so that they " are co-heirs, incorporated in the same body, and co-sharers in the promise, in Christ Jesus, through the gospel " (Eph. 3:6). This means that the gentiles already share in the heavenly riches and the hidden glory of Christ, so that they can hope for the complete glory which is to come, which will be revealed only at his second coming. The manifold riches of Christ's glory are already visible in the brilliant light which the gospel preaching casts over the gentiles and the divine life which they receive from Christ's sacraments. In Christ, God's eternity reaches into our passing world; the influence of his divine life makes itself felt in this world of death. Christ is our " hope of glory," so that our life on earth and the history of the world as a whole are preserved from absurdity. In Christ the world has hope.

The Essence of St. Paul's Exhortation: "Promoting Christ" (1:28)

28 *It is him we proclaim, in that we exhort every human being and instruct everybody in all wisdom, to present every human being perfect in Christ Jesus.*

St. Paul proclaims Christ to the gentiles. This is an " official " proclamation which takes place in public, before the whole world; Christ is proclaimed Lord and Saviour of the gentiles. However, proclaiming Christ also includes the duty of apostolic exhortation; Christ must be Lord over people's hearts and all their decisions. " Promoting Christ " (Luther), therefore, includes for St. Paul the duty of admonishing people; everyone must be duly instructed, so that the Apostle can exhibit " every human being perfect in Christ Jesus." Christ himself is the goal of this process which is aimed at leading the faithful to perfection; he must be reproduced in them to perfection. And yet they already live " in " him in some mysterious way. St. Paul is always anxious to insure that what one is and what one does, what one knows and how one behaves are in harmony. The proclamation of the gospel is always an invitation to repentance, as it was in our Lord's preaching (Mk. 1:15).

This verse also demonstrates how acutely conscious St. Paul was of his responsibility for his converts. Presenting the faithful as perfect human beings in Christ also means presenting them before the divine Judge (cf. 2 Cor. 11:2). One day St. Paul will have to present them before Christ and he wants to be sure that he will have no cause to be ashamed of them before the Lord. " Indeed, who is our hope, our joy, our glory, in the presence of our Lord Jesus Christ when he comes? Is it not you? Yes, you are our pride and our joy " (1 Thess. 2:19–20). That is why he insisted that his converts should put the gospel into practice. A purely theoretical Christianity, a Christianity which was confined to faith alone, would be an abomination to St. Paul, as it was to our Lord himself who said, " It is not the man who calls me ' Lord, Lord ' that will enter the kingdom of heaven, but he who does the will of my Father in heaven " (Mt. 7:21).

St. Paul, therefore, regards the commission given him by God as including three important duties; to preach the gospel to all men, which reveals a wonderful secret to them; to see that his converts lead a Christian life; and to suffer in their place and on their behalf. So he is engaged in a constant struggle for his communities, as he now goes on to explain.

St. Paul's Struggle on Behalf of the Community (1:29—2:7)

His Anxious "Striving" (1:29—2:1)

29 *For this I make every effort, as I strive, relying on God's power which works so effectively in me.*

St. Paul spares no pains to achieve his purpose, to exhibit the faithful "perfect in Christ Jesus." He often speaks in his epistles of these labors in the service of his ministry, among which he includes the hard work he did with his hands as a tent-maker. "Remember, brothers, all my toil and labors: night and day, I was busy with manual work, to avoid being a burden to you; that was how we preached the gospel to you" (1 Thess. 2:9). He also counts among his labors his sufferings as an apostle in the course of his missionary work (1:24). They are accompanied by unremitting and anxious striving in worries of every conceivable kind, both interior and exterior. St. Paul realizes he has no defense against these, but he endures them courageously, relying on God's power which is active in him. In this battle, he fights as "a good soldier of Christ Jesus" (2 Tim. 2:3); he does not fight with earthly weapons, but with weapons which are "powerful in God's sight to destroy every bulwark; we destroy fallacious reasonings and everything that raises itself against true knowledge of God; we make every mind a prisoner in the obedient service of Christ" (2 Cor. 10:3f.).

He regards those who work with him as his fellow soldiers. Euodia and Syntyche "have fought for the gospel at my side, as . . . fellow-laborers of mine" (Phil. 4:3). His converts owe him the support of their prayers in this battle; "Brethren, I implore you by our Lord Jesus Christ, and by the love of the Spirit, to fight for me with your prayers to God on my behalf" (Rom. 15:30). This struggle is not against "flesh and blood"; not against earthly armies; it is against (diabolical) "principalities and powers, against those who rule over the darkness in this world, against evil spirits in the heavenly world" (Eph. 6:12). At the end of his life, St. Paul could say, "I have fought the good fight; I have finished the course; I have kept the faith" (2 Tim. 4:7).

Christianity is not a pious idyllic existence; it is a lifelong struggle which demands constant self-renunciation from him who has the faith to fight it. "Every contestant practices complete restraint. They do it to receive a crown which passes, while we do it for one which is eternal" (1 Cor. 9:25).

[1]*Indeed, I must tell you what a battle I am fighting for you and for those at Laodicea, and [for] all those who have never seen me, . . .*

When St. Paul says this, he is obviously thinking of the spiritual battle which he is waging on behalf of the communities. It is a battle of prayer (1:3, 9) and of apostolic exhortation (1:28) which he fights on their behalf. Prayer is a struggle with God and Satan for souls. St. Paul fights:

That the Communities May Have a Fuller Understanding of Christ's "Secret" (2:2–3)

[2]*. . . so that your hearts may be strengthened, united in love, and for all the full wealth of insight, for the knowledge of God's secret which is Christ,* [3]*in whom all the treasures of wisdom and knowledge are concealed.*

St. Paul tells the Colossians about his striving in prayer (2:1a), so that their hearts may be strengthened. When he says this, it is clear that he has in mind the dangerous heresies which were circulating in Colossae (2:8, 16–23). It took courage to resist them and their supporters; the heresies made presumptuous claims which were intended to overawe those who adhered to the "old" faith. The Colossians must stand firm shoulder to shoulder, in order to resist them; they must form a closely-knit community of love. Only a community which is united by the bond of genuine brotherly love is proof against heresy. In a community where there is no love, all the doors are open to heretics and sectarians.

The heresy in question at Colossae concerned the secret of Christ's salvation and so, in his letter and by his prayers, St. Paul strives for the gift of greater penetration and understanding of this divine secret, which is Christ. An immature and imperfect faith which wavers between truth and falsehood (Eph. 4:14) only too easily falls prey to a heresy which claims to offer wisdom and understanding.

In St. Paul's mind, Christ is "the secret revealed to us by God," purely and simply; in him "all the treasures of wisdom and knowledge are concealed." There is no doubt that, in this phrase, St. Paul deliberately stresses the word "all." Christ is the fullness of all wisdom and knowledge, and this is directed against the heresy at Colossae (2:4, 8). "Indeed, in him, you have become rich in every form of learning, every type of knowledge" (1 Cor. 1:5). A person who has once really understood Christ has no wish to look for another kind of wisdom or a different treasury. Anyone who has learned to recognize him by faith knows the secret of Christ's place in the universe and in history (1:15–20, 26f.; Eph. 1:10; 3:3–12), as well as the ultimate secret of man's destiny, which is revealed in the "second Adam."

"It remains for us, who once bore the mark of the earthly [Adam], to bear the mark of the heavenly [Christ]" (1 Cor. 15:49). Christ is the solution of all the world's "riddles." As yet, the treasury of wisdom and knowledge is still "stored up" in him, but it is accessible to the knowledge which is accompanied by faith, because faith enables a person to penetrate it. For the world of unbelievers, on the other hand, these treasures are still hidden.

It is in the Saviour's heart that these treasures of wisdom and knowledge are stored up for those who have faith.

Another object of St. Paul's striving is:

That the Community May Be Preserved from Heretics (2:4–5)

4 I speak of this, so that no one may lead you astray with high-flown speech. 5 For, even though I am absent in my body, I am with you in spirit and the sight of the order and firmness of your faith in Christ makes me joyful.

St. Paul now comes closer to the real point at issue in this epistle. It is clear that there were some people in the community who were causing confusion by their own peculiar form of "high-flown talk" and St. Paul was very worried about what was going on. Even though he cannot be present in person, he is there in spirit, so that he can make due provision by means of his apostolic authority and love. His word, whether written or spoken, is binding on the community; as long as they maintain unity with him, their steadfastness in the faith can be assured. Informed presumably by Epaphras, St. Paul "rejoices" that the Colossians' faith in Christ is well ordered and firm. This has an almost military sound; the battle line of faithful soldiers has not yet been broken; the faith they inherited from the apostles is still a firm bulwark.

An Exhortation to Live in Christ According to the Tradition (2:6–7)

[6]*As you have now received the Lord Christ Jesus, walk in him . . .*

For St. Paul, faith in Christ is not the product of "free thinking"; it is contained in the apostolic tradition with which the Colossians had become acquainted through the activity of missionary preachers, and which they have received. Speaking more accurately, the content of tradition is Jesus Christ himself; together with the faith, the Colossians received Christ (cf. Eph. 3:17). They received him especially as their "Lord," the Lord in whose service they now stand; he gives them a share in his wisdom and glory.

That is why the Colossians must walk in him; they must model their entire religious and moral lives on him. There is a definite Christian "mode of life" which has its roots in the gospel and is handed on in the form of "tradition" within the Christian communities from generation to generation, together with the faith. This preserves them from making misguided concessions to the spirit of any particular age.

[7a]*. . . rooted and built up in him . . .*

A root must strike deep into the soil, if it is to nourish the tree and make it firm. The soil on which a Christian community stands is Christ; it is rooted in him as in its life-giving source. It is also built up on him as a holy "temple dedicated to the

Lord " (Eph. 2:21). This foundation has been laid once and for all; there can be no other (1 Cor. 3:11).

7b. . . *firmly established in the faith in which you were instructed, . . .*

The Colossians must be " established " in the faith, if their faith is to be able to hold its ground against the heretics. This faith is firmly established in them when they hold by it according as they " were instructed." The content of this " instruction " is the " tradition," which it explains and from which it draws practical consequences for the Christian life (1:28; Eph. 4:20f.). Anyone who has listened to this teaching in a spirit of submission and understanding is firmly established in the faith and proof against heresy.

7c. . . *overflowing with gratitude.*

Really genuine faith must bear fruit in gratitude; it must " overflow " with it. Faith includes insight and in the immediate context of this epistle this means insight into Christ's secret of salvation. The man who has faith realizes that he has been redeemed (Rom. 8:24; Eph. 2:5, 8), so that he never ceases giving thanks (1:11f.). Obviously the best way of doing this is in the celebration of the Eucharist.

A First Warning against Heresy (2:8)

St. Paul has now prepared the Colossians sufficiently and so he comes to the real point at issue, the heretical doctrine which was causing such harm among them. There is no doubt Epaphras had told him all about it. He now warns them against it briefly, for the first time.

8 *See to it that no one carries you off as his prize by means of " philosophy " and vain lies [which follow] human traditions and the world elements, not Christ.*

We could say that a heretic preys upon a community; he tries to capture people, treating them as so much spoil. For this purpose, the heretics at Colossae tried to pass their views off as a " philosophy "; this was bound to make a good impression with certain people; it sounded as if it meant a higher form of wisdom and understanding. Paul and his fellow laborers used appeal to the tradition handed down by the apostles and the early church (2:6). In the same way, the heretics too appealed to " tradition," but St. Paul was quick to stigmatize it as " human tradition "; it was not founded on divine or apostolic authority. In his judgment, which was binding on the community, their so-called " philosophy " was nothing more than a collection of " vain lies " by which the community must not be deceived.

St. Paul now describes the content of this heresy briefly as adoration of the elements of the world. We are no longer in a position to say exactly what this meant; in any case, it led to a denial of Christ's supremacy as the " Head " of everything created and redeemed. It was with good reason that St. Paul had emphasized the creation and redemption of everything through Christ, in the " Christological hymn " in 1:15–20. There are no exceptions; the redemption of the world comes from him alone. It is clear that the heretics did not believe this; they attributed a redeeming role to the " elements of the world," that is, to some form of created beings. This gravely prejudiced Christ's role in the world of creation and redemption. It is not

" according to Christ," as St. Paul says literally, and he gives further reasons for this in the following verses.

The heresy prevalent at Colossae was due ultimately to the ever-recurrent temptation to succumb to the tremendous impression made by the " powerfulness " of the world, its vastness, its concrete visibility, and its apparent eternity, all of which " force " themselves upon men. In this sense, the warning St. Paul had for the Colossians is valid for all time.

Salvation and Redemption through Christ Alone (2:9–15)

The heretics at Colossae denied Christ's exclusive primacy by demanding that Christians should worship the " elements of the world." That is why St. Paul takes such pains to set forth Christ's role in this epistle. He had already done this very forcibly in the " Christological hymn " in 1 : 15–20 and he returns to the same theme once more in 2:9–15, where he introduces a number of new viewpoints.

Christ, the Plenitude of Deity (2:9)

9For the fullness of the divinity lives bodily in him . . .

If the " elements of the world " are to be worshipped, as the heretics maintain, this is because they believe these elements share in the divine being, in the " fullness " of deity. This would mean that they had an indispensable role to play in the salvation of the world. St. Paul emphatically rejects such an idea by stating categorically that the whole plenitude of deity is in Christ "bodily." It dwells in him really and truly. Christ cannot be forced to share his divine plenitude with the elements of the world, as the heretics believe. The world is created; as such, it does not share God's being; it is "profane." To pay it religious veneration is either fanaticism or idolatry, and this can take many different forms.

"Completed" in Him (2:10)

10 *. . . and you are completed in him, for he is the head of every kind of authority and power.*

The Christian community at Colossae, as everywhere else, forms part of the church which, according to Ephesians 1:23, is the "body" of Christ, "the fullness of him who everywhere and in all things is complete." That is why St. Paul can tell the Colossians that they too "are completed in him [Christ]." It is especially by means of the sacraments that they share in the fullness of the divine life and grace of their heavenly Lord. From the moment of baptism they have entered into a communion of life with Christ (Eph. 2:5); he is the Head "on whom all the body depends" (Col. 2:19). In and through Christ they are enabled to escape the fateful sentence of death which hangs over the whole world.

Therefore, they have no need to have recourse to the "elements of the world"; in point of fact, these are incapable of granting victory over death. Christians live in union with Christ over whom death has no more power (Rom. 6:9); he is Lord even over death. Christ is the head of every kind of authority and power, as St. Paul reminds his readers. As their fountainhead, Christ enjoys the mastery over all dominions; as a result of being raised up to God's throne in heaven, he is placed " high above all principalities and powers and virtues and dominations " (Eph. 1:20-22). Those who have been baptized have no more need to be afraid of the demons or powers, or to pay them reverence. Fear of the demons is a pagan attitude. Christ protects Christians from them, if they only remain true to their " Head."

"Circumcised" in Him (2:11)

11*You have also been circumcised in him with a circumcision which was not performed by human hands, but by putting off the natural body, by Christ's circumcision, . . .*

According to Genesis 17:11–13, God commanded Abraham, " You shall circumcise the flesh of your foreskins, as a sign of the covenant between me and you. Generation after generation, every male child shall be circumcised when it is eight days old . . . So must my covenant be visible in your flesh as an eternal covenant." In the new covenant which was sealed with the blood of Christ (Lk. 22:20; 1 Cor. 11:25), the spiritual circumcision which Christ bestows, which is accomplished at baptism, takes the place of the external rite of circumcision in the old law. This involves putting off the natural body which means that " our old self has been crucified with him so that the body which was given over to sin might be destroyed and we might be slaves of sin no longer " (Rom. 6:6). In this way, baptism marks the birth of a " new self " (Col. 3:10; Eph. 2:15) which belongs completely to Christ and his kingdom.

United with His Burial and Resurrection (2:12–13)

[12]*. . . since you were buried with him in baptism . . .*

According to St. Paul's teaching, baptism is above all a dying. But it is not a lonely and purely " private " dying; it is a dying " in union with " Christ. " Do you not know that all of us who were baptized into Christ were baptized into his death? We have been buried with him into his death . . ." (Rom. 6:3f.) By baptism, therefore, a Christian shares in a mysterious manner in Jesus' death. In a certain sense, he is buried with him in the tomb. St. Paul takes this as referring to " our former nature," which was subject to sin and death (Rom. 6:6). The powers which bring death have lost their dominion over those who are baptized, provided that they do not voluntarily surrender themselves to them again by sin.

This view of baptism as the sacrament whereby we are taken up into Christ's death sets our human life and destiny in a completely new light. Our real death takes place at the very beginning of our life on earth—in baptism. All the sufferings and sorrows of life and especially physical death which brings them to an end are only the way in which this overwhelming event which has already taken place works itself out in our personal lives. The Christian life is a continual dying whereby we are taken up into Christ. In this way, the sufferings the faithful have to endure in this life are relieved of their apparent absurdity; bodily death above all, which marks the end of our lives, no longer seems a catastrophe. Far from it! When it is accepted in a spirit of submission, it is only the Christian's final Yes to something which has already been accomplished in principle in baptism. This gives us a completely new view of our human lives: "For me, life means Christ; death is a gain" (Phil. 1:21). "Dying men, and see, we live (2 Cor. 6:9). St. Paul is entitled to say this, because not only have we died with Christ, but we have also been raised from the dead with him.

12b. . . *in which you have also been raised up with him, by faith in the power of God who raised him from the dead.*

A Christian's real death takes place at the beginning of his life, but this death brings with it at the same time true life. As well as a sharing in Christ's death, baptism involves also a mysterious resurrection from the dead in union with Christ (cf. 3:1; Eph. 2:6). We know "that Christ who has risen from the dead cannot die any more; death has no more power over him" (Rom. 6:9). From the moment of baptism, the faithful already have a share in the indestructible life of their heavenly Lord. In this way, the world of divine life which is to come, which we call "heaven," already reaches into the earthly life of the baptized. This too throws a completely new light on the lives of Christians here on earth.

Christ is the Christians' real being; everything takes place in Christ and in union with Christ. This is the expression St. Paul prefers to describe the mystery of our Christian life. "I am alive, but it is not really I any more, it is Christ who lives in me" (Gal. 2:20). "Once a man is in Christ he is a new creature. His old self has vanished. See, a new self has arisen" (2 Cor. 5:17). The only thing is that the new life which a Christian receives in baptism is still "hidden away with Christ in God" (Col. 3:4a). Faith knows that it is real and appreciates the miracle of God's power which takes place at baptism, although our earthly life is still subject to death. Faith crosses the threshold of death; it knows and recognizes that the miracle which God works at baptism is real. " If we have died with Christ, we believe that we shall also live with him " (Rom. 6:8).

13*You were dead because of your sins and the fact that your flesh was uncircumcised, but he gave you, too, life together with him, having first forgiven us all our sins.*

Once more St. Paul tells the Colossians that they have really been raised " from the dead " in baptism, in order to make them appreciate it fully. This time, moreover, he makes it clear in what their former lifeless state consisted; they were dead in their sins. " Sin offers death for wages " (Rom. 6:23), including physical death (cf. Rom. 5:12, 15, 17). St. Paul is thinking especially, however, of the " real " death which sin brings, separation from God and his indestructible life. This was the death to which the Colossians were subject in their pagan days. In baptism, God has done away with that nature which was " all uncircumcised " and raised them " to life " again in union with Christ, so that they " who were dead have come to life " (Rom. 6:13); they now share the divine life of the risen Christ.

Sharing in Christ's life presupposes that their sins have been forgiven, and God in his goodness does this on account of Christ's death on the cross. In this way, the cause of man's subjection to death was removed and he could be received into the world of Christ's life.

God Canceled the Deed Which Excluded Us, through Christ (2:14)

14*He erased the debit note which affected us, whose terms were against us, and canceled it completely by nailing it to the cross.*

St. Paul is speaking figuratively here; the sins of mankind, we could say, had been entered in the debit column of an account where they bore witness against us. God now nailed this deed to Jesus' cross, just as a proclamation of their guilt used to be fixed to the cross of condemned criminals where it could be read by all (cf. Jn. 19: 19–22). As the Lamb of God who bore the guilt of the whole world, Jesus took our sins on himself on the cross and died in our stead. God " made him who knew no sin into sin for our sakes " (2 Cor. 5: 21). On the cross, Christ canceled the deed which excluded us, which listed all our sins. " Look, this is the Lamb of God; this is he who takes away the sin of the world."

He Disarmed the Powers through Him (2:15)

15 *He disarmed the powers and dominions and put them to shame by triumphing over them in him.*

The consequences of Jesus' death on the cross are worldwide. It is not only that the sins of mankind were wiped out; the powers and dominions were disarmed by him. With these words, St. Paul returns once more to the real point which he wishes to make. The Colossians were still afraid of diabolical powers in the world, just as they had been when they were pagans, despite the fact that Christ is already " the fountainhead from which all dominion and power proceed " (2: 10). They did not yet realize this sufficiently, or they would not have allowed themselves to be confused by the heretics. The dominions and powers have been " put to shame " through Christ; their powerlessness was demonstrated when Christ who had been crucified was raised from the dead. In this way, God triumphed over Satan's power, in Christ.

Since then the cross has been the great sign of God's victory in the world.

A Second Warning against Heresy with More Precise References to Its Teachings (2:16-23)

St. Paul had already given his readers a first warning against heresy in 2:8. Most of the detailed explanations he has given up to this are offered with this heresy in view, to a greater or lesser extent. This is true especially of what he has to say about Christ's role in the world of creation and redemption, and also of what he says about the salvation which God has reserved for the Colossians. Now, however, he speaks in detail of the false doctrine which was threatening the community. Epaphras will have informed him of the danger and given him a close account of the heresy involved with all its peculiarities. In verses 16–23, St. Paul makes a number of allusions which give us some idea, even today, of what it was like, although much remains obscure. It seems to have been an extraordinary mixture of the gospel and various elements of Jewish and pagan origin. Its effect was to deprive the Christian message of any reality or power.

It is part of the church's duty of watchfulness to safeguard the "true path of the gospel" (Gal. 2:5–14) in Christian communities and preserve them from heresy.

Their Superstitious Practices (2:16–17)

16*So let no one criticize you because of food or drink, or because of any feastday, new moon, or sabbath day.*

St. Paul now attacks the heresy in question directly. He alludes to some of its prescriptions which refer primarily to what people eat or drink. It seems likely that the heretics maintained that certain foods were " unclean," whereas Christ had declared them all clean (Mk. 7: 19) and added, " Nothing enters a man from without which can defile him; it is what comes out of a man that defiles him " such as " malicious thoughts, adultery, murder, stealing, impurity, greed, malice, lying, debauchery, envy, blasphemy, pride, and folly " (7: 15, 22).

In addition, the heretics prescribed that certain days and times should be observed, presumably in connection with the worship of the " elements of the world." It is possible that they had divided the days superstitiously into those which were propitious and those which were not, as many people still do today; superstition is not dead yet. The arrogance of the heretics was visible especially in the fact that they presumed to " criticize " their fellow members in the community who did not share their views. A heretic always behaves arrogantly.

17 *These things are [only] shadows of what was to come, the body belongs to Christ.*

Everything that is provisional and transitory, such as food and drink, falls short of what is to come; it can do nothing to hasten it. What is to come, for St. Paul, is Christ purely and simply (cf. 3: 9) and even a Christian's body belongs to him (cf. 1 Cor. 6: 15), while food and drink are merely a form of nourishment (1 Cor. 6: 13). They have no significance for man's future salvation. This is true also of the days and times which the heretics superstitiously regard as being favorable or adverse to man's salvation. " These things are only shadows "; they have nothing to do with real salvation which depends on Christ alone.

The "Mystery" Character of the Heresy (2:18)

18 No one must condemn you, while taking pleasure himself in " humility " and the worship of angels, boasting of " visions," puffed up without cause by his own worldly thoughts; . . .

St. Paul once more contents himself with a number of brief allusions to the teaching of the heretics. From his remarks, however, we can conclude that it involved some kind of mystery-cult, such as was widespread at the time in various forms. People were " initiated " into these esoteric cults and hoped through them to acquire higher knowledge of the heavenly beings and their affairs. It is clear that the catch-word " humility " played a role in the Colossian variety of these cults, but it is impossible to make out what exactly it referred to. Similarly, an extraordinary and exaggerated " worship of angels " was important. Presumably this consisted in paying greater reverence to certain angels than to Christ. As often happens in such cases, the heretics appealed to alleged " visions," in which they claimed this " higher " knowledge was communicated to them.

St. Paul will have none of it. He sees in it all nothing more than the inflation which is caused by worldly thoughts, the presumption which refuses to be content with the "ordinary" gospel. The gospel is not an esoteric doctrine; on the contrary, it is proclaimed publicly before the whole world. "What I say to you in darkness, you must speak in the light; what is whispered in your ear, you must proclaim from the housetops" (Mt. 10:27). Moreover, the gospel is concerned with our everyday lives; that is why it must prove itself in practice and especially in serving our neighbor. It must not be left to dreamers, aesthetes, fanatics, and the like.

Separation from the "Head" (2:19)

[19]*. . . in this, such a person fails to remain united with the head by which the whole body is cared for and held together by means of sinews and bonds, while growing with God's growth.*

It is part of the teaching of the gospel that salvation comes exclusively from Christ alone. This was exactly what the heretics at Colossae denied; they made salvation depend on meaningless observances. They did not maintain unity with the "Head", Christ, from whom alone his "body", the church, draws its power of heavenly growth. The whole body is supplied by him; there is no need to look for other sources of salvation, which are not such in reality or which themselves draw their life from Christ, such as the angels.

A Warning against Their "Prescriptions" (2:20–21)

[20]*If you have died with Christ to the elements of the world, why do you allow prescriptions to be imposed on you, as if you [still] lived in the world?* [21]*[Such as:] Do not touch this, do not taste that, do not handle those!*

The heretics at Colossae had exacting prescriptions and strict rules for their followers. St. Paul mentions some of them, and we should note his ironical tone, "Don't touch this, don't taste that, don't handle those!" These prescriptions clearly refer to certain types of food (2:16); in addition, they betray a superstitious and magical approach to various material things ("Don't handle those"), perhaps including the domain of sex. Presumably people were afraid of becoming "unclean" or "bewitched" by some diabolical influence, as a result of such contact.

For a Christian, the world is stripped of its magical and divine character; he sees it for what it really is, God's creation, in which there is nothing unclean. "And God saw all that he had made, and it was very good" (Gen. 1:31). Moreover, everything was created through Christ and for him, as St. Paul has already reminded the Colossians (1:16). Christ is the Lord of all. St. Paul also reminds them that "by dying with Christ" in baptism, they have abandoned the "elements of the world" from which they had expected salvation, in their pagan days. Christ is their Master now and he alone brings them salvation; the whole plenitude of deity really dwells in him. If they allow themselves now to be burdened with the heretics' "prescriptions," it means that they are going back to what they had rejected, when they were baptized. It means that they are allowing their former paganism to re-enter by the back door, so that they water down the gospel and deny the power of baptism.

It is part of the gospel message that the world is "profane"; God and the world must not be confused.

These Are Only Human Prescriptions (2:22–23)

22a *Yet all this is meant to be used and consumed.*

The gifts of creation have nothing to do with the devil; there is no reason why we should be suspicious of them; they are good and are intended for our use. "See, I am giving you all the seed-bearing herbs which are found in the whole world, and every tree on which there is fruit which yields seed; this is to be your food" (Gen. 1:29). "Do you not understand that nothing which enters a man from outside can make him unclean, because it makes its way, not into his heart, but into his belly, and so is cast into the sewer" (Mk. 7:18f.). This is the "prosaic" view which Jesus takes, and a Christian must take the same view.

[22b]*These are human prescriptions, the teaching of men* [23]*who, it is true, lay claim to "wisdom," accompanied by an [extraordinary] show of piety, "humility," and unsparing corporal mortification [which in reality is] quite worthless, [only serving] to satisfy their own ego.*

With their doctrine and their various prescriptions, the heretics lay claim to a special "philosophy." They are convinced that they are on the right track to a solution of the "riddles of the world." Above all, however, they adopt a pose of more fervent piety. It is clear too that they and their followers practiced exaggerated corporal mortifications, which always give the impression of great piety. Their influence over some of the Colossians was all the more seductive for that. St. Paul is not impressed. On the contrary, he castigates their views and their regulations as the prescriptions and teachings "of men," which have no divine authority whatever, such as he himself could claim for his teaching. They are quite worthless for salvation such as it is offered to a Christian. Ultimately, they are based on pious self-deception and serve only "to satisfy their ego" that is, their earthly and pagan tendencies. They have nothing to do with the gospel.

There is a great difference between piety and "pietism"; self-deception in religious matters will always be a danger to Christianity. The heresy which formerly existed at Colossae in Asia Minor belongs to the past, but it contains elements which can always reappear in Christianity, in one form or another, and bring the "gospel truth" into danger. What St. Paul has to say about it, the arguments he adduces against it are of perennial interest to the church. He fixes the church's gaze decisively on Christ; he alone brings salvation and he is the world's hope.

ST. PAUL'S DIRECTIONS FOR THE LIFE OF THE CHRISTIAN COMMUNITY (3:1—4:6)

In the first chapter St. Paul explained the mystery of Christ. He did so quite clearly with the situation of the Christian community at Colossae constantly in view. There the community was threatened by a particularly dangerous heresy. In the second chapter he now gives practical directions for the Christian life of the community. These directions are equivalent to general principles of the Christian life and are important for the church in all ages. As is clear from 3:1, they must be understood primarily as practical consequences of the mystery of baptism. Once they have received baptism, Christians " must consider themselves as people who are dead to sin, but living for God, in Christ Jesus our Lord " (Rom. 6:11).

St. Paul likes to use the conjunction " then " to introduce the section of his letters which is devoted to practical living, and Col. 3:1 is no exception. This use of the word " then " shows us immediately that St. Paul regards his apostolic exhortations as practical consequences of the theoretical presentation of the Christian life which precedes them. Being a Christian must result in behaving as a Christian.

Lift Up Your Thoughts Above (3:1–4)

1If, then, you have been raised up with Christ, seek what is above where Christ sits at God's right hand.

For St. Paul, baptism is no mere pious ceremony; it is a great mystery, the most important thing in a Christian's life (2:11–13). At baptism the old self dies and a new self is raised from the dead, which is united "with Christ." Because, "then," this is what happens at baptism, a Christian's interior gaze must be re-orientated; it must be resolutely lifted "above." It is there that the new center of meaning of the Christian community and of every individual Christian is to be found, the center which is Christ. Since his Ascension, he has been raised up to God's right hand, and it is there that those who seek him will find him.

2*Fix your thoughts on what is above, not on what is on earth!*

St. Paul inculcates the necessity for this new outlook a second time, but he uses a different expression. In the preceding verse, he had spoken, literally, of "seeking" what is above; here he speaks of the necessity of being "heavenly-minded" (in one's judgments and thoughts). A Christian's thoughts and judgments should be centered "in heaven," that is, on Christ who has been raised to glory, and not on what is earthly. The whole of creation has already been renewed in Christ. This undoubtedly involves a radical "reappraisal of one's values"; it demands an ever greater degree of detachment from all that is earthly on the part of a Christian. However, this does not mean that a Christian must neglect his duties and obligations in this world (cf. 1 Thess. 4:11f.); it means that he must not allow himself to become lost in his earthly occupations, as if these were the beginning and end of everything. A Christian fulfills his obligations in this life with his gaze resting on Christ, his Lord and his hope.

3*Remember you have died and your life is hidden with Christ in God.*

St. Paul bases his demand that we should resolutely lift our gaze above on the fact that we have already " died " in baptism (cf. 2:12), as he reminds us. It is there too that we receive the new life which is a share in the life of the risen Christ (2:13) who is now enthroned in heaven. For the moment, therefore, this life is concealed from our earthly gaze; like our Lord himself, it is " hidden away with Christ in God."

St. Paul does not mean by this that a Christian leads a " double " life, an " inauthentic " existence in this world and an " authentic " existence in heaven. What we cannot see with our earthly eyes is the mysterious union of life which exists between a baptized person and Christ, the hidden source of his life. Christ himself is his source of life (3:4). A Christian lives by the mystery which is Christ; consequently, his gaze must be fixed on him.

4 *When Christ, your life, is revealed, then you also will be revealed with him in glory.*

Christ will be made manifest at his second coming, at the end of the world. Then he will leave the concealment of heaven and manifest himself as the real Lord of the world, for whom everything was made (1:16) and in whom everything in heaven and on earth is " summed up " (Eph. 1:10). It is then that the " life " which God gave us at baptism will cease to be invisible and hidden. Then it will appear in all its glory and even our bodies will share in it, so that we shall be completely " molded into the image of his Son " (Rom. 8:29).

In these verses, St. Paul draws his readers' attention to the ultimate goal of their lives and of all history, before beginning his exhortation proper. Turning their thoughts to what, for a

Christian, is the only reality provides a powerful motive for their lives as Christians. The mystery of Christ in his life should give a Christian strength to live a life worthy of him. St. Paul shows us what this means in practice; it means refusing to spend oneself on " what is earthly."

Put Off the Old Self (3:5–9)

5 Therefore, you must kill everything in you that still belongs to the earth, fornication, impurity, passion, evil desire, and greed, which is a form of idolatry.

These words of St. Paul show us what he means by earthly-mindedness. It is not the attitude of a person who is filled with wonder and grateful love for creation and its gifts which he condemns; such an attitude is quite compatible with " heavenly-mindedness." What he condemns is rather subjection to the sinful " concupiscences of the flesh," of which he names a whole list, including impurity. A Christian must " deaden " these passions, because they are incompatible with his new life in Christ. " Therefore, sin must no longer reign in your bodies, that you should obey its desires. You must not make your limbs instruments of wickedness at sin's disposal. On the contrary, put yourselves at God's disposal, as men who have risen from death to life . . ." (Rom. 6: 12f.).

St. Paul stresses greed particularly. This is the unruly " desire for more " which is never satisfied; it is always on the look out for even greater gains which are far in excess of the necessaries of life. This is contrary to the gospel; it is an " idolatry," because a devotion and reverence which are really due to God alone are paid to earthly things, money and possessions. Our Lord tells us, " Be careful and keep yourselves clear of all greed " (Lk. 12 : 15).

[6]*It is such things which provoke God's anger.*

God's vengeance is revealed in his judgment. Jesus wishes to save his followers from God's vengeance which is to come (1 Thess. 1 : 10), but it will infallibly come " on the unbelievers." No one should try to fool himself or anyone else about this (Eph. 5 : 6).

[7]*And your conduct, too, was once confined to such things, when you [still] lived your life in them.*

As a Jew, St. Paul strongly condemns the gentiles' former lives (cf. Rom. 1 : 18–32), with special reference to their immorality and general degradation. He reminds the Colossians too of their pagan past. A Christian does not close his eyes to his past life; he does not suppress or conceal the sins he has committed. On the contrary, he is full of gratitude and never forgets God's infinite goodness and mercy by which he called him from death and sin to his own life and light (1 : 21f.; Eph. 2 : 1, 5).

[8]*Now, however, you too must put all that away from you, anger, rage, malice, blasphemy, and the abuse which comes from your lips.*

" Now " everything must be changed, for " now " the great " mystery of Christ " (4 : 3) has been revealed to the Colossians (1 : 26f.). " Now " Christ has reconciled them with God by his death on the cross (2 : 22). " Now " that they belong to Christ, they must cast off the vicious habits which belong to the past.

Once more, St. Paul gives a whole list of the vices whose irreligious character was particularly visible. They are for the most part serious offenses against fraternal charity and include also foul-mouthed utterances. A Christian's tongue is given to him to praise God and bless his fellow men (3:16; Rom. 12:14). With our tongues "we praise our Lord and Father, and with them we curse our fellow men who are made in God's image. Blessing and cursing come from the same mouth. My brothers, that should not be so" (Jas. 2:9f.).

9 *Do not deceive one another with lies; you have put off the old self and its practices . . .*

St. Paul mentions lying especially which should never be found among Christians. In the whole Bible, lying is condemned with particular forcefulness. "Lying lips the Lord cannot abide" (Prov. 12:22). "Lying lips were ever the soul's destroying" (Wisd. 1:11). When the devil utters falsehood, "he is only uttering what is natural to him; he is a liar and the father of lies" (Jn. 8:44).

Lying is typical of the "old self," which the Colossians have put off at baptism, with "the habits that went with it." A Christian must be a friend of the truth; lying is a sign of interior corruption.

Clothed in the New Self (3:10–11)

10 *. . . and put on the new self which is being renewed for knowledge in the image of him who created it.*

At baptism a Christian puts off the old self and puts on the new self. In his pagan days, in the past, he wore the dress of the old, sinful Adam; now, as a Christian, he must wear the dress of the new Adam, who is Christ. The white baptismal robe is a visible symbol of this change.

Adam was created originally in God's image (Gen. 1:26), but this divine likeness was obscured by the fall. It is now being renewed in Christ who is God's true likeness (Col. 1:15), although it will remain hidden from our bodily eyes until the resurrection of the dead. "We bore the image of the earthly man, and in the same way we shall bear the image of the heavenly [Christ]" (1 Cor. 15:49).

The renewal of our likeness to God at baptism brings with it a new knowledge. This is primarily the closer knowledge of good and evil, which the old self did not have. A Christian is in a much better position to know God's will than the old pagan self (cf. 1:9; 4:12). In addition, the new self knows the great mystery which St. Paul sums up in the following verse with the words, "Christ is everything and in everyone." A baptized Christian is once more in a position to recognize in other men his own brothers, which Cain and his descendants were no longer capable of doing (cf. Gen. 4:24). In this way, baptism paves the way for a new race of men in a new world.

11 *Here there is no [more] Greek or Jew, circumcised or uncircumcised, no more barbarian, Scythian, slave or freeman; on the contrary, Christ [is] everything and in everyone.*

There are various differences between human beings and distinctions are made, for example, on a religious, racial, or social basis. In antiquity, things were no different than they are today. The Jews recognized the one true God, while the gentiles adored a multitude of gods. This created a "barrier" between them

(Eph. 2:14), which led to "hostility" in religious matters. The Greeks in their turn looked with contempt on the "barbarians" who did not share their language and culture. Society as a whole was divided into slaves and freemen. At baptism, however, we Christians "have all been baptized into a single body, whether we were Jews or Greeks, slaves or freemen" (1 Cor. 12:13). "All of you who have been baptized into Christ, have put on Christ. It does not matter any more whether a person is a Jew or a gentile, a slave or a freeman, a man or a woman. You are all one in Christ Jesus" (Gal. 3:27f.). In other words, we all form part of the "one new humanity" which Christ creates in baptism (Eph. 2:15).

As the new and final Adam, Christ obliterates all the distinctions which characterized the ancient world; he restores to man the divine likeness he once enjoyed. In the Christian community are congregated all those who have put on the new self; there the old differences and distinctions are meaningless. The church invites all men to enter the kingdom of God, no matter what class or race they belong to. This new community which embraces all men and all races is already visible in the liturgical assembly; there all have "access to the Father" (Eph. 2:18) on equal terms. In the church, therefore, the world to come, in which all men will be brothers, is already clearly visible. It is one of the specific duties of Christianity in our day to proclaim loudly the unity of all men and all races in Christ.

A Picture of the New Self (3:12–16)

In the following section, St. Paul sketches an essential portrait of the new self which the baptized Christian must try to achieve. It is a picture of a perfect Christian.

Tender Compassion and Kindness (3:12)

[12]*As God's chosen people, holy and beloved, clothe yourselves with heartfelt compassion, kindness, humility, gentleness, and patience.*

The fact that all men are members of one great family of brothers, which is manifested and demanded by our relationship with Christ, calls for a completely new attitude towards his fellow men on the part of a Christian, an attitude which is in direct contrast to that described above (3:8). Christians are "God's chosen people, holy and well beloved." They are "chosen" because God has called them to faith in the gospel; they are "holy" because they are members of God's people; and they are "well beloved" because they have been redeemed by Christ's blood. Therefore, they must be clothed with heartfelt compassion for all those who endure suffering in this world; they must show kindness, a kindness which is ready to understand and forgive, humility which gives way before another, gentleness which listens sympathetically, and patience which waits quietly for that which is not mature to become mature.

At the back of St. Paul's demands stands the image of the new humanity as it is visible in a unique way in Jesus of Nazareth.

Readiness to Forgive (3:13)

[13]*Bear with one another and be forgiving to one another, when anyone has a reproach to make against another. As the Lord has forgiven you, so you too [must forgive].*

Everyone has his own peculiarities, both pleasant and unpleasant, and one person easily gets on another's nerves. We often judge according to our likes or dislikes. St. Paul, however, does not hesitate to demand that we should bear with one another. This means putting up with our fellow men precisely in their unpleasant characteristics and constantly overcoming our antipathies. This is especially important in situations where people live in close contact with one another as, for example, in marriage.

"We are betrayed, all of us, into many faults" (Jas. 3:1), especially into faults against our fellow men. That is why St. Paul calls for readiness to forgive on the part of Christians, as our Lord himself had done; "Even if [your brother] offends you seven times in the day, and comes back to you seven times with the words: 'I am sorry,' you must forgive him" (Lk. 17:4). As the motive and model for such readiness to forgive, St. Paul cites God's example. He has forgiven us, through Christ (cf. 2:13; Eph. 4:32). God's forgiveness puts us too under obligation to forgive and makes it possible for us to do so. His attitude is a model for the faithful.

Charity and Peace (3:14–15a)

[14]*In addition to all this [practice], charity; charity is the bond [of unity] which brings to perfection.*

"All this," all that St. Paul has just mentioned, must be crowned with charity. The various forms of Christian behavior which have already been recommended must be inspired by charity. It is charity which unites all the virtues and makes them perfect.

When individual Christians, without exception, make charity their goal, Christ's body, the church, grows "with a growth which is divine" (2:19). St. Paul's own goal in his instructions is to "present every human being perfect" (1:28; cf. 4:12) which, in the light of 3:14, can only mean making them perfect in the practice of charity. It is this which is the perfection of a good Christian.

15a *And may the peace of Christ reign in your hearts. Indeed, you are called to this in the unity of one body.*

The peace which Christ gives is not the peace which the "world" gives (Jn. 14:27). Christ's peace is founded on reconciliation and love (Col. 1:20); its source is God's heart and Christ's. This is the peace which must govern the hearts of the faithful. This is the peace to which they are called; all those who have been baptized form a holy community, the "body of Christ," which is filled by Christ (1:18; 2:9f.; Eph. 1:22f.). There must be no fighting or discord in this community. It is only when these conditions are realized that the church can appear to the world as God's great sign, which is worthy of credence. In our days especially, all men and all races must see the church as a place of peace and an invitation to it. The gospel is God's great message of peace to the world (Eph. 2:13–17).

Gratitude (3:15b)

15b *And be grateful!*

This is a concise piece of advice, but its content is nonetheless rich. A Christian is a person who gives thanks (1:3, 12; 2:7; Eph. 5:20); he gives thanks to God for the salvation he has granted him, and he gives thanks to his fellow men for the love and help he has received from them. An ungrateful person is incapable of forming part of a community. Gratitude, on the other hand, makes possible a give and take which lasts forever and makes a person happy. "He praised God aloud, and threw himself at Jesus' feet . . . to thank him" (Lk. 17:15f.). Gratitude towards God is expressed especially by praising him aloud (3:16c).

The Spiritual Life of the New Self (3:16)

In this verse, St. Paul mentions in a few brief words three things which should play a special part in the spiritual life of the new self. We almost get the impression that there are definite references here to the liturgical worship of the community as it existed in the time of St. Paul.

16a*May Christ's word live continually in you in abundant measure; . . .*

Christ's word, for St. Paul, is "at the same time the word he himself brings." "We thank God unceasingly that you listened to God's word which you heard from us, not as if it was a human message, but as a message from God, which it really is. As such it is also active among you who believe" (1 Thess. 2:13). Christ's word, which St. Paul proclaims, is a priceless treasure which has been entrusted to him; it is identical with the "truth-giving message of the gospel" which the Colossians received (1:5). It is no mere transitory word; it is intended to remain with them; it must "have its shrine" in the hearts of the Colossians and of all Christians, in "all its wealth." There it must grow and bring forth fruit (1:6).

Christ's word comes to the community above all in the liturgical assembly. There it is repeatedly proclaimed and expounded, so that people may be familiar with it and it may bring forth fruit in their daily lives. It must be listened to with respect and gratitude, if it is to "have its shrine" among us.

16b. . . *instruct and encourage one another in all wisdom.*

The heretics too claimed that their words were words of wisdom (2:23). But St. Paul means a different wisdom; he is thinking of the wisdom which is a fruit of Christ's word. Anyone who listens to Christ's words in the right spirit will receive that wisdom which will enable him to "instruct" and "advise" his fellow men in the right spirit too.

"The wisdom from above is pure, first of all, but it is also peaceful, gentle, obedient, full of pity and good dispositions; it is free from partiality and hypocrisy" (Jas. 3:17). This is the kind of mutual encouragement which Christians should exchange among themselves.

16c*In your gratitude, sing psalms, hymns, and spiritual songs in your hearts for God.*

The spiritual music characteristic of the Christian community is the expression of the Christian's gratitude towards God who has given him his salvation (cf. Eph. 5:19). In this verse, St. Paul certainly has in mind the liturgical assembly of the community and the songs and hymns which are sung there. These are "spiritual" songs, because the Holy Spirit himself is at work in them and fills those who are assembled with his presence. Ultimately, the liturgy is a work of the Holy Spirit in the church. That is why the celebration of the liturgy gives rise to that atmosphere of holy calm which is characteristic of Christian worship and distinguishes it from any merely worldly festivity.

Spiritual music such as this helps to build up the community and reveals it as a holy society of brothers. In this way, liturgical worship becomes a source of strength which enables Christians to overcome the difficulties of their daily lives.

The community which sings is already identical with the rejoicing bride of the Lamb. "I heard a great multitude singing jubilantly, like the roar of many waters and the roll of heavy thunder: Alleluia; The Lord our God, the Almighty, has entered on his reign. Let us rejoice and exult and pay him honor. The Lamb's wedding is at hand, his bride is ready" (Apoc. 19:6f.).

Do Everything in the Lord's Name and Giving Thanks to God (3:17)

17a *And whatever you do, in word or in activity, [do it] all in the name of the Lord Jesus . . .*

"Whatever you are about" refers to the advice St. Paul has given his readers up to this and also, we may be sure, to all that he has not said in so many words. A Christian's every word and action should be accomplished, invoking the Lord's name; this is the advice St. Paul gives, by way of summing up what he has said. Nothing should be excepted from this advice, not even the "profane" activities of a Christian. Jesus Christ is Lord, not only of the community, but of the whole of creation. The Christian community professes faith in his name and by invoking it everything is directed towards him, "through whom and for whom everything was created" (1 : 16). In this way, everything is sanctified and subjected to Christ's dominion.

17b. . . *and give thanks to God the Father through him.*

St. Paul has already called upon his readers to show their gratitude repeatedly. However, this verse is no mere repetition. Here he says clearly that all thanks must be given to the Father "through him," through Christ; it is through him that everything was created and redeemed and everything should be done while invoking his name. This gives rise to a relationship of thanksgiving between the community and God, in Christ, in which Christians realize that God is their "Father"; in Christ, they are united in communion with him for all eternity. Offering their thanks "through Christ," Christians approach the Father in a spirit of adoration, which is the basic disposition of Christianity as a whole. This becomes a matter of experience, even here and now, as often as they meet for the great Christian expression of thanks, the celebration of the Eucharist.

A Domestic Program (3:18—4:1)

The " household rules " which we meet so often in the New Testament are intended to govern the social obligations of Christians in the various states of life, with particular reference to their everyday lives. The program laid down for slaves is out of date in modern times; at the same time, however, St. Paul's exhortation to fulfill our daily duties faithfully is valid for us too.

Wives (3:18)

18 *You who are wives, be submissive to your husbands, as is expected of you in the Lord.*

The pagan moralists of antiquity used to offer similar advice, but St. Paul's instructions are distinguished from theirs by the addition of the important phrase, "as is expected of you in the Lord." These words mean a lot; as baptized persons, married Christians are "in Christ"; he is their Master, their Lord, and their Judge, even in their married life. In all circumstances, a Christian looks to the will of his Master which he fulfills joyfully.

Husbands (3:19)

19 *You who are husbands, love your wives and do not be harsh with them.*

St. Paul's demand that husbands should love their wives makes it clear that the relationship of "submission" between husband and wife (3:18) must not be understood as a slavery. The husband must respond to his wife's submissiveness with love; harshness towards her in thought, word, or deed, would be the opposite of love. In Ephesians 5:21–35, St. Paul gives a more detailed description of what married love should be like. Christ himself is its model; he gave himself up on behalf of his bride, the church.

Children (3:20)

20 *Children, obey your parents in everything, for this finds favor in the Lord.*

No exceptions are made to the obligation of obedience towards one's parents, and children owe the same obedience to both their father and mother. This is a gracious sign of serving the Lord. St. Paul undoubtedly had the fourth commandment in mind.

Fathers (3:21)

21 *Fathers, do not harm your children, so that they will not lose heart.*

In antiquity, a father's authority was virtually unlimited, but St. Paul limits it here with the important warning not to harm the child psychologically in exercising it. Real education is aimed at bringing out the best in a person; it does not destroy the child's self-confidence by being harsh. A child must be able to obey with a heart which is free from constraint.

This detailed program of family life gives us a good picture of St. Paul's idea of the family. For him, it is made up of husband and wife who together with their children form a community which is based on love, reverence, and obedience, in God's sight. This is one of the finest elements of Jewish tradition which St. Paul brought into the church.

Slaves (3:22–25)

22 *You who are slaves, obey your earthly masters in everything,*

not serving the eye, to find favor with men, but in simplicity of heart and the fear of the Lord. 23*No matter what you are doing, do [it] from your hearts, as [something done] for the Lord, not for men;* 24*you know indeed that you will receive the inheritance as a reward from the Lord. Christ is the Master you serve.* 25*The man who does wrong will reap the reward of his crime. There is no favoritism.*

No one would dare to offer slaves the advice St. Paul gives them here, if he were not convinced of three things: that there are no human preferences with God; that there is a retribution which is eternal; and that all men are brothers in Christ (3:11). St. Paul did not demand the abolition of slavery, but he wrote to Philemon asking him not to treat Onesimus, his runaway slave, "as a slave anymore," but "as something better, as a beloved brother. He already is this to me in a special way, and still more to you, both as a human being and in Christ" (Philem. 16). Such statements had consequences which were bound to lead to the abolition of slavery in the nations which were converted to Christianity.

Masters (4:1)

1*You masters, treat your slaves justly and fairly. You know, surely, that you, in your turn, have a master in heaven.*

Masters, too, have obligations towards their slaves. They are bound to care for their temporal and spiritual welfare and they will have to account for it before the heavenly Judge.

The recommendations which St. Paul makes for the organization of the Christian household are far more comprehensive than those offered by the moralists of antiquity. The gospel affects our entire earthly existence, although it does not disturb the natural order of things.

Final Exhortations (4:2–6)

Prayer and Intercession (4:2–4)

2 *Persevere in prayer and be on the watch with it, with thanksgiving.*

St. Paul himself was a man of prayer (1:3, 9) and it was his wish that the members of the Christian community should also be devoted to prayer. "Never cease praying" (1 Thess. 5:17), "pray at all times in the spirit; keep a constant watch, interceding for all the saints" (Eph. 6:18). The incessant prayer which the Christian community offers is a sign of their wakefulness, which is conscious of the "evil time" which is to come (Eph. 6:13), when the anti-Christian power of Satan will be concentrated for a final assault on God's elect (cf. 2 Thess. 2:3–12). But they are conscious too of the day of salvation, when their Lord will return, to save his community and hand everything over to the Father. It is this consciousness which enables Christians to live "in expectation of the happy fulfillment of their hope and the glorious coming of our God and Saviour, Jesus Christ" (Tit. 2:13). Therefore, they cannot afford to sleep like the rest; they must remain sober and keep watch (1 Thess.

5:6). The day of the Lord comes like a thief in the night. The prayer of the Christian community is primarily a prayer that the Lord will come soon, "Come, oh Lord" (1 Cor. 16:22). It is precisely because Christians offer their prayer in the conviction that the Lord is coming that it must always be accompanied by thanksgiving. A Christian does not thank God merely for the salvation by which he has already benefited (1:12-14); he thanks him also for giving him knowledge of what is to come, the triumph of Christ and final redemption. The principal occasion for such thanksgiving is the celebration of the Eucharist.

3Pray also for us, that God will open a door for us to preach the word, to proclaim the mystery of Christ because of which I lie in chains, 4so that I can make it known as it is my duty to preach it.

St. Paul himself intercedes with God for his communities (1:3b) and so he writes, "You, too, must help us with your prayers" (2 Cor. 1:11), especially now that he is in prison. He is not resigned to abandoning his mission because of that; in whatever situation he found himself, he did his best to proclaim the "revelation of Christ," which is nothing less than the "gospel revelation" (Eph. 6:19). He regarded this as the great duty God had laid upon him. "I want you to know that my position has resulted in promoting the gospel. The whole imperial bodyguard and all the others realize that it is for Christ's sake I am in chains. The majority of the brothers in the Lord were encouraged by my bonds and are more daring than ever in their fearless preaching of God's word" (Phil. 1:12-14). In addition, however, a missionary needs the prayers of the Christian community.

Relations with Others (4:5–6)

5*Guide your attitude wisely with respect to those who are outside [the community]. Make the most of your time!*

The communities which St. Paul and his fellow laborers had founded lived in pagan surroundings, " in the midst of a warped and perverse age," in which they should shine out, " beacons to the world " (Phil. 2:15). Pagans regard Christians with criticism and suspicion, but their lives must be such as to have the effect of an eloquent sermon on them; in particular, their lives must act as a gentle invitation to the pagans to open their hearts to Christ's message. Jesus had commanded his disciples, " Let your light shine before men, so that they will see the good you do and give praise to your Father in heaven " (Mt. 5:16). St. Peter, too, exhorts Christians: " Be always ready to give everyone his answer. . . . Do it gently, respectfully, with a good conscience, so that those who revile your good behavior in Christ will be put to shame in their calumny " (1 Pet. 3:15f.). A Christian's life must have a missionary effect.

Then, too, they must grasp their opportunity eagerly. The " opportunity " is fleeting, a short respite which will come to an end with Christ's second coming. The mission which constitutes the church's most important duty on this earth must not be frustrated by the sinful behavior of Christians. Every moment of this life is valuable and must be employed in the service of the gospel.

6*Your words must be always seasoned with salt and gracious, so that you know how you must reply to each one.*

The " words " in question here are the words involved in the

Christians' missionary efforts. This is primarily a message which brings salvation and only secondarily a proclamation of judgment (cf. Mk. 1:15). That is why it must be "gracious." The Greek term for "gracious" (*charis*) is that used for "grace." The gospel is the message of God's grace.

This missionary message must be seasoned with salt; it must be penetrated with the power and zest of the gospel which can cure the world's corruption. A message which relied only on flamboyant eloquence would not be a missionary message. "My speech and my preaching did not make use of impressive words of wisdom. Instead, they were accompanied by proofs of the Spirit and power, so that your faith should rest, not on human wisdom, but on God's power" (1 Cor. 2:4f.).

Many of the people a Christian meets are honestly looking for the truth; they expect that the gospel and the church should answer their questions. The answers a Christian gives will convince these questioners only if they are "gracious, and seasoned with salt," as is characteristic of God's word.

With this exhortation, St. Paul comes to the end of his advice for the Colossians.

THE CLOSE OF THE LETTER
(4:7-18)

CONCLUSION
(4:7–18)

Tychicus and Onesimus Will Give Them News of Paul (4:7–9)

[7]Tychicus will tell you everything about me, a beloved brother, a true minister, and fellow bondsman in the Lord.

It is only with this verse that St. Paul comes to speak of his personal circumstances. As a true apostle of Jesus Christ, the spiritual state of the Colossians is far more important to him. At the same time, however, his fate at the moment is not without importance for the community at Colossae; the battle he is fighting is on behalf of the faithful.

Tychicus, who was probably a native of Ephesus (cf. Acts 20:4; 2 Tim. 4:12), accompanied St. Paul on his last journey to Jerusalem, together with a number of others. He may have traveled with the apostle as the representative of some community, to bring the offerings of the gentile Christians to the first community at Jerusalem. Now he is returning to Asia Minor and will bring news of St. Paul to Colossae.

St. Paul describes him as a "dearly loved brother"; all Christians are brothers in Christ. He also calls him a "true minister," because he was in the Lord's service and had proved himself in it; and a "fellow bondsman" who, like Epaphras (1:7), had dedicated himself to spreading the gospel, so that he was St. Paul's companion. Sharing the same faith and the same ministry in the Lord's service made them all a closely knit community of brothers.

8 *That is precisely why I have sent him to you, that you may know how we stand, and he may strengthen your hearts . . .*

The news which Tychicus will give them about St. Paul's circumstances will strengthen their hearts. The apostle can say this with the firm assurance that the news of his situation will strengthen the Colossians in their loyalty to him, and so to the gospel; on the other hand, this will be a reinforcement against heresy.

9 *. . . and, besides him, Onesimus, a faithful and well loved brother, one of yourselves. They will tell you about all our circumstances here.*

Onesimus is the slave who had run away from Philemon and taken refuge with St. Paul (cf. Epistle to Philemon). St. Paul calls him his "well loved brother"; for him, he is not a slave. The Colossians seem to know him ("he is of your own number") and if St. Paul now sends him to them, together with Tychicus, so that both of them can bring them news of his imprisonment, this is a proof of the great confidence he places in him. But it is also an example which he sets them; the Colossians must realize that all those who have been baptized are brothers in Christ and that the old class distinctions have lost their meaning as a result.

Greetings from the Others (4:10–14)

St. Paul now comes to the greetings which close his letter. Before sending the Colossians his own greetings, he mentions those who send their regards with him and he sends special regards to some of his own acquaintances. The six persons who send greetings with him are all fellow laborers in his missionary work. The long list of greetings in St. Paul's epistles (cf. especially Rom. 16) have a profound meaning. They show the deep consciousness of their own brotherhood which filled the Christian communities. It was only right that they should be filled with such a consciousness, together with a lively awareness of the responsibility of each individual for the whole community.

10 *Aristarchus, my fellow prisoner, and Barnabas' cousin Mark, about whom you have [already] received instructions, send you their greetings. When he reaches you, make him welcome.* 11 *And also Jesus who is called Justus. [They are] the only ones from the circumcision who are working with me for God's kingdom. They have been a comfort to me.*

Aristarchus was a Macedonian (Acts 19:29) from Thessalonica (Acts 27:2); he shared St. Paul's imprisonment voluntarily. Mark was from Jerusalem; he accompanied St. Paul and Barnabas on their first missionary journey, but left them en route, which led to a temporary disagreement with St. Paul (cf. Acts 13:5–13; 15:37–39). St. Paul now recommends him to the Colossians, to whom he bore instructions. Together with these, St. Paul mentions a certain Jesus who was called Justus ("The Just Man"), of whom we know nothing further.

At this period, Mark and Jesus Justus were the only Jews who helped St. Paul in his missionary endeavors (cf. Philem. 24). The Jewish Christians caused him a lot of trouble, but Mark and Jesus Justus supported his apostolic activity, although they were Jews too. In this way, they were a "comfort" to him, not merely in his personal situation at this time, but because in their loyalty to him they contributed to the peace and harmony of the church. They sought Christ's interest, not their own (cf. Phil. 2:21).

12Epaphras your countryman sends greetings. A slave of Christ Jesus, he spares no pains in his fervent prayers for you, that you may be perfect and completely filled with everything that is God's will. 13I can testify on his behalf that he puts himself to great trouble for you, together with those at Laodicea and Hierapolis.

It was Epaphras who had brought the Colossians knowledge of the gospel (1:7) and informed St. Paul about the community's circumstances (1:8). As a faithful "slave of Christ," he shared St. Paul's missionary anxiety for them; together with him, he strove to promote their spiritual welfare by his prayers (cf. 1:9, 29). He had the same purpose as St. Paul, to make the Colossians perfect Christians (cf. 1:28). This included the hope that they would be full "of all that is God's will." This does not refer merely to their moral lives; it refers also to the knowledge of God's saving will, to all the great things which God has in mind for them (cf. 1:9; Eph. 1:9).

Epaphras' anxiety also extends to the Christian communities in Laodicea and Hierapolis. He even suffers from them, as St. Paul can testify. It is quite possible that he had encountered difficulties in these communities, perhaps on the part of the heretics. St. Paul vindicates him in the eyes of these communities by referring to his genuinely apostolic conduct which shows that his missionary efforts are inspired by pure motives. In this way, he commends his loyal fellow worker and gives him a certificate of honor.

[14]*Luke, the beloved physician, and Demas greet you.*

Luke, the evangelist and author of the Acts of the Apostles, had accompanied St. Paul on his last journey to Jerusalem and afterwards to Rome (Acts 21 : 1f.; 27 : 1ff.). We can be sure that he also shared his imprisonment at Caesarea. He was a doctor by profession and must have often been of service to St. Paul in this capacity, as he was not strong. In this way, St. Luke used all his talents in the service of the gospel. We know nothing further of Demas, but he must have been known to the Colossians.

This exchange of greetings on the part of all St. Paul's companions gave rise to and maintained a bond of heartfelt brotherhood between the missionaries and the Christian communities, which is part of the essence of the church.

Greetings to the Brothers and Sisters and Final Instructions (4:15–17)

[15]*Greet the brothers at Laodicea, especially Nymphas and the church in her house.*

It is only with this verse that St. Paul sends his own greetings, first of all to the community at Laodicea. This is followed by a name which may be that of a man or a woman; it obviously means a married couple in whose house the community or a part of it assembled for public worship. This demanded strength of character, love, and unselfishness. It indicated a consciousness of responsibility for the brothers and sisters who formed part of the same community.

16 *And when this letter has been read to you, make sure that it is also read in the community at Laodicea, and* [*get*] *the one to Laodicea, so that you too can read it.*

St. Paul has one more important direction to give; the Colossians must see that his letter to them is read out to the Laodicean church too, and that his letter to Laodicea, which was soon lost, was also read at Colossae. This shows that St. Paul himself regarded his epistles not as " private letters," but as " official " documents which were not directed merely to one particular church. The problems he treated in them were constantly recurring in one form or another and the solutions he proposed remain decisive for all time. Similarly, the exhortations he makes as an apostle are valid indefinitely.

The place where his letters would be " read out " was obviously the liturgical assembly of the community. This circumstance served to underline the "official " character of his epistles and soon led to collections of them being formed in the different churches. In the course of time, they acquired a standing similar to that enjoyed by the writings of the Old Testament which were also read out and expounded in the liturgical assembly. In this way, St. Paul's epistles came to form part of the church's " sacred scripture," like the gospels.

His letters are also " sacred scripture " for us; what he wrote to the Colossians so long ago is still " read out " to us in the liturgical assembly. In them, God's Spirit himself speaks to us; it was he who guided the apostle when he wrote his letters.

17 *And tell Archippus: Pay attention to the ministry which you have received in the Lord and fulfill it perfectly.*

We have no idea who Archippus was or what the " ministry " was which he had to fulfill. This warning of St. Paul's, however, shows us that every " duty " in the church is committed to a person " in the Lord." This means that Christ himself is the origin of it; it is he who bestows all duties and all offices in the church (cf. Eph. 4:11-16) and an account of them must be rendered to him. Therefore, Archippus and anyone else who has been entrusted with a duty in the Christian community must be careful to fulfill it.

Greetings in St. Paul's Own Handwriting (4:18a)

18a [*And here is*] *Paul's greeting, in my own hand. Remember my bonds!*

As in other letters, St. Paul adds here a greeting written in his own hand; the rest of the text was written down by his secretary. The community must see his own handwriting and recognize in it an intimate proof of his attachment to them. His last request, " Remember my bonds," is intended to remind them once again of the suffering which he endured for the gospel. Ultimately, it was because of his chains that he was most closely united with his communities, while they were united with him by their refusal to forget that he was in chains. His last request to the Colossians is still fulfilled in the church at the present time, if we also refuse to forget all those who are "in chains."

Good Wishes (4:18b)

18b *Grace [be] with you!*

St. Paul's good wishes are brief and to the point, but despite their brevity, they mention the essential thing, without which the Christian community cannot exist, God's grace. Moreover, the word "grace" on St. Paul's lips means a lot; the blessing, help, and all the prosperity which God gives his community in Jesus Christ, the Colossians as well as Christians in our own day.